D1462821

THE HAMILTONIAN VISION,

1789–1800

Also by William Nester

The Revolutionary Years, 1775–1789:
The Art of American Power During the Early Republic

The Jeffersonian Vision, 1801–1815:
The Art of American Power During the Early Republic

THE
HAMILTONIAN
VISION,
1789-1800

The Art of American Power During the Early Republic

WILLIAM NESTER

Potomac Books
Washington, D.C.

Maps by Chad Blevins.

Library of Congress Cataloging-in-Publication Data
Nester, William R., 1956–
     The Hamiltonian vision, 1789–1800 : the art of American power
during the early republic / William Nester. — 1st ed.
         p. cm.
     Includes bibliographical references and index.
     ISBN 978-1-59797-675-6 (hardcover : alk. paper)
     ISBN 978-1-59797-882-8 (electronic)
1. United States—Politics and government—1789–1797. 2. United
States—Politics and government—1797–1801. 3. Hamilton, Alexander, 1757–1804. 4. Federal government—United States—History—
18th century. I. Title.
     E311.N47 2012
     973.4—dc23

                                                            2012012977

Potomac Books
22841 Quicksilver Drive
Dulles, Virginia 20166

First Edition

10 9 8 7 6 5 4 3 2 1

Contents

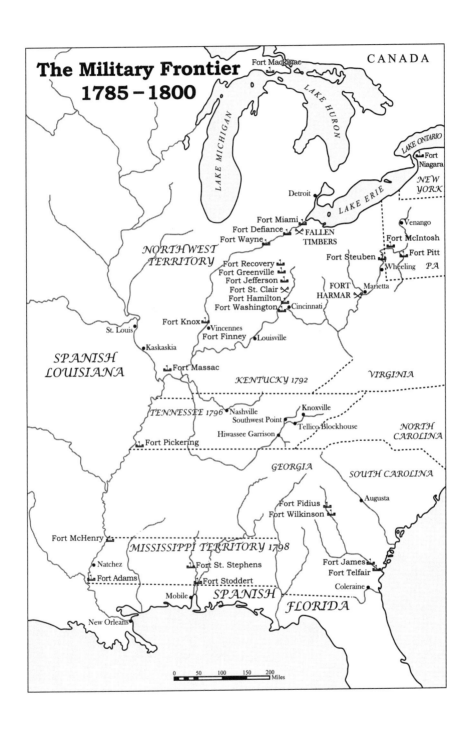

The Military Frontier
1785–1800

CANADA

Fort Mackinac

LAKE MICHIGAN

LAKE HURON

LAKE ONTARIO

Fort Niagara

NEW YORK

Detroit

LAKE ERIE

Fort Miami

Fort Defiance

Fort Wayne

FALLEN TIMBERS

Venango

Fort McIntosh

NORTHWEST TERRITORY

Fort Recovery

Fort Greenville

Fort Jefferson

Fort St. Clair

Fort Hamilton

Fort Washington

Cincinnati

Fort Steuben

Fort Pitt

Wheeling

PA

FORT HARMAR

Marietta

Fort Knox

Vincennes

Fort Finney

Louisville

St. Louis

Kaskaskia

SPANISH LOUISIANA

Fort Massac

KENTUCKY 1792

VIRGINIA

TENNESSEE 1796

Nashville

Southwest Point

Hiwassee Garrison

Knoxville

Tellico Blockhouse

NORTH CAROLINA

Fort Pickering

GEORGIA

SOUTH CAROLINA

Augusta

Fort Fidius

Fort Wilkinson

Fort McHenry

MISSISSIPPI TERRITORY 1798

Natchez

Fort St. Stephens

Fort Adams

Fort Stoddert

Mobile

SPANISH

FLORIDA

Fort James

Fort Telfair

Coleraine

New Orleans

0   50   100   150   200
Miles

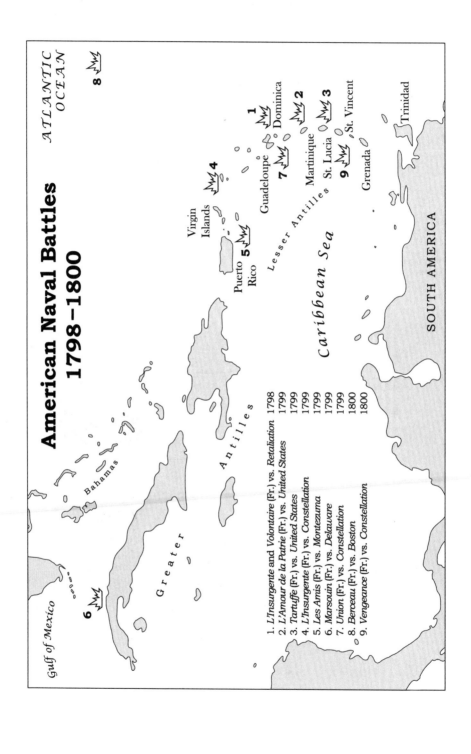

American Naval Battles
1798–1800

ATLANTIC OCEAN

Gulf of Mexico

Bahamas

Greater
Antilles

Virgin
Islands

Puerto
Rico

Lesser Antilles

Caribbean Sea

Guadeloupe
Dominica
Martinique
St. Lucia
St. Vincent
Grenada
Trinidad

SOUTH AMERICA

1. L'Insurgente and Volontaire (Fr.) vs. Retaliation   1798
2. L'Amour de la Patrie (Fr.) vs. United States   1799
3. Tartuffe (Fr.) vs. United States   1799
4. L'Insurgente (Fr.) vs. Constellation   1799
5. Les Amis (Fr.) vs. Montezuma   1799
6. Marsouin (Fr.) vs. Delaware   1799
7. Union (Fr.) vs. Constellation   1799
8. Berceau (Fr.) vs. Boston   1800
9. Vengeance (Fr.) vs. Constellation   1800

Acknowledgments

I cannot express enough my deep gratitude to Elizabeth Demers, senior editor at Potomac Books, first for wanting to publish my Art of American Power series and then for carefully editing each book. She made numerous corrections and wonderful suggestions that greatly strengthened my books. I also owe a great deal to Julie Kimmel, for her meticulous copyediting, and Aryana Hendrawan, my production editor. It is such a great pleasure to work with such wonderful people and outstanding professionals as Elizabeth, Julie, and Aryana.

Introduction

The Inauguration

The inauguration of America's new government got off to a shaky start.[1] At times the voice and hands of George Washington, who had proved himself to be a man of unflinching courage on a dozen battlefields, trembled noticeably as he was overcome with emotion on his first day as president.

Those in charge of the proceedings in New York City on April 30, 1789, designed a day of events in which pomp and festivity framed the solemnity of the central event. At nine o'clock that morning the city's churches opened for services during which the ministers extolled the virtues of America in their sermons and led prayers for the prosperity of the young republic and the wisdom of its president.

At half past noon George Washington stepped out of his lodging into the bright, warm sunshine. He was dressed in a sober brown coat, knee breeches, a tricorne hat, a white silk shirt, stockings, and gleaming silver-buckled black shoes. His long, graying hair was lightly powdered and tied back. He paused briefly to acknowledge the cheers of the crowd that had eagerly awaited his appearance then climbed into a canary-yellow carriage drawn by six white horses. A marching band and a company of blue-coated soldiers preceded the carriage down streets lined with joyful throngs.

The procession halted in the square before Federal Hall, the former city hall that had been renovated by the brilliant architect Pierre-Charles L'Enfant, who a decade later would design the layout and public buildings of Washington City. Federal Hall was a soaring two-story building with a steep slate roof topped by a tall cupola. Four square pillars lined the recessed space to the front door; four round pillars lined the balcony above. Within, on the first floor, a huge reception hall was flanked by wings with floor-to-ceiling windows. A grand marble staircase joined the floors. The House of Representatives would sit in a chamber on the ground floor, and the Senate would convene on the floor above them.

With musicians and soldiers lining either side of the hall's entrance, Washington stepped out of the carriage. The cheers of ten thousand people packed into the square reached a deafening roar as the new president briefly nodded his appreciation then strode toward the hall. Vice President John Adams led the delegation waiting to greet Washington. Together they disappeared into Federal Hall and a minute later reappeared on the second-story balcony. There, after somehow briefly hushing the crowd, Robert Livingston, New York's chancellor, administered the oath of office of the president of the United States. With a slightly quavering hand on the Bible and barely audible voice, Washington repeated the words, adding at the end, "so help me God." The cheers erupted again as the president bowed slightly to the crowd. He and his entourage strolled back inside and into the Senate chamber. There, in a trembling voice, George Washington delivered his inaugural address.

Even then the ceremonies were not yet done. Washington was ushered back to the carriage, and the procession slowly made its way through the packed streets to St. Paul's Church on Broadway for a thanksgiving service and Te Deum. Only after that were Washington and scores of dignitaries and their wives conveyed to a mansion for the grand feast and ball that lasted far into the night.

In light of how vital his role had been in helping frame and ratify the Constitution, atop his service as Washington's most brilliant aide during the war, it may come as some surprise that Alexander Hamilton played no part in the official inaugural ceremonies.[2] He and his wife, Betsy, simply watched the public segment of the ceremony from the balcony of their Wall Street townhouse and attended the ball that evening. Hamilton was not part of the transition team, nor had Washington yet tapped him to join his government. However, Hamilton would soon be the president's point man in proposing and pushing for congressional approval initiatives designed to revolutionize American economic and military power.

In that extraordinary age of intellectuals and statesmen, Alexander Hamilton was perhaps the most brilliant, and like Benjamin Franklin, he personified the self-made man. He was born out of wedlock on the tiny island of Nevis in the West Indies. By the time he was in his late teens, the island's elite recognized his genius and in 1772 sent him to the Elizabethtown Academy in New Jersey. After graduating, he entered King's College, now Columbia University, in New York City. As tensions swelled with Britain, he wrote liberal pamphlets, joined the Sons of Liberty, and formed an artillery battery. After fighting broke out he fought valiantly at the battles of White Plains, Trenton, and Princeton. Impressed by his extraordinary intelligence, drive, and courage, George Washington asked Hamilton to join his staff. Throughout most of the war, Hamilton not only helped run the army but also wrote most of Washington's speeches and reports. During the Yorktown campaign, Washington finally succumbed to the lieutenant colonel's long-standing pleas that he be given a field command. Hamilton led his troops in a daring night attack that captured a key British redoubt.

With peace, Hamilton became a prominent voice for financial reform, a strong central government, a partnership between the public and private sectors in developing the economy, and the abolition of slavery. He was a delegate to the Convention and achieved renown for defending and explaining the Constitution, along with James Madison and John Jay, through the Federalist Papers; Hamilton wrote fifty-one of the eighty-five essays.

Hamilton not only was a theorist but was just as brilliant at practicing statesmanship, nation-building, and politics. When he took office as America's first treasury secretary, the economy was locked in a vicious cycle of debt, inflation, stagnation, and poverty. Within a few years, his policies transformed the economy into a virtuous cycle of growth, exports, innovation, financial stability, and prosperity. Hamilton consolidated the congressional and state debts into one federal debt that was funded with revenues from trade tariffs and excise taxes. He established the dollar as America's currency and the First Bank of the United States to manage the nation's money supply in a way that created and distributed ever more wealth to ever more Americans. And those were just his economic reforms. He was the most powerful voice in shaping the Washington administration's policies toward an array of other pressing domestic and foreign challenges, including building the foundations for a professional army and navy.

No founder achieved so much and is less well known. At least everyone who handles a ten-dollar bill knows how Hamilton appeared even if they know little or nothing of what he did. Yet even a portrait can be deceptive if it freezes that person's well-coiffed appearance at one fleeting time of his or her life. Hamilton was five foot seven inches in height, about average for that era. He was lean as a youth but thickened with age. His light reddish-brown hair began to thin, recede, and gray during his thirties. He had a florid complexion that deepened with excitement. He did not consider himself handsome and regretted his rather close-set violet-blue eyes and long pinched nose. Yet he was well aware that he exuded a natural animal energy and magnetism that drew men and women alike to him, and he did not hesitate to exploit that to his advantage. He may have suffered from manic depression, with exuberance predominant during his younger years and melancholy more frequently afflicting him as he aged. Nonetheless, he was noted for his elegance and grace on virtually all occasions.

He was a voracious reader who especially enjoyed history and political philosophy. He was an outstanding writer. In his youth, he dabbled in poetry that ranged from philosophical to romantic to bawdy. His first political essays were published when he was twenty, and thereafter he produced volume after volume of some of the most powerful and eloquent treatises ever written. He has been falsely accused of favoring an aristocracy and even a monarchy for the United States. Actually, he always espoused a republic dedicated to protecting the natural rights and promoting the prosperity of all Americans.[3]

As a child he suffered poverty and the stigma of being a bastard whose father fled his family when he was ten. That experience can drive someone to be selfish, greedy, uncaring of others, or outright larcenous. It had the opposite effect on Hamilton. He was generous throughout his life and did what he could to help those in need. He was scrupulously honest and never succumbed to the temptation to enrich himself from public funds or insider trading. Likewise most people who grow up in a slavocracy become fierce defenders of their "right" to own and exploit their fellow human beings. Not so Hamilton, who from his youth hated slavery, believed that blacks were the intellectual and moral equals of whites, and sought to abolish that evil system.

With his charm, wit, learning, and ebullience, Hamilton made friends easily. Unfortunately as his career advanced, he made enemies just as easily. That was partly owing to the jealousy of those who were just as ambitious but lacked the brilliance and luck that vaulted him to be George Washington's most trusted adviser during the War for Independence and his first term as president. Atop that were genuine philosophical differences over what to do about all the challenges facing the United States, with none more vital than the new republic's institutions, duties, and powers. But Hamilton transformed ever more opponents into enemies by eviscerating them with razor-sharp prose that exposed the entrails of their greed, ignorance, illogic, dishonesty, and hypocrisy.

He suffered no illusions about human nature. Speaking from experience, he found most men governed by their "prevailing passions" of "ambition and interest," which made them "vindictive and rapacious." He was not any more optimistic when regarding the political savvy of the common man: "The people are turbulent and changing. . . . They seldom judge or determine right."[4]

As Hamilton mulled such sentiments, he may well have had himself in mind. His passions were not confined to championing an independent and ever more prosperous and powerful United States. His Achilles' heel was women. Martha Washington playfully named her tomcat Hamilton for his namesake's ardent pursuit of any maidens who appeared at her husband's headquarters. In several surviving letters to his friends, he boastfully alludes to his prowess and endowment in seducing many a pretty woman, maiden or not.

Alas, after marrying he persisted in enjoying such liaisons despite the obvious danger to his family and career. He had a brief but torrid affair with Angelica Church, his wife, Betsy's, beautiful, vivacious, and worldly sister. He then fell for a classic honey trap with the irresistible Maria Reynolds, who threw herself in his arms with a tale of an abusive husband who had gambled away her dowry and left her penniless. That willing cuckold soon appeared with a fistful of love letters proving their infidelity and demanded hush money. Thereafter Hamilton would empty his wallet and integrity repeatedly into Reynold's eager hands. Rumors of the affair, blackmail, and payments swirled and reached the ears of Hamilton's political enemies, who charged him with diverting Treasury funds to silence his lover's husband. In August 1797 Hamilton replied with a public letter in which he confessed his affair but insisted that he had not diverted a penny of public money to his blackmailer. The sex scandal ruined his future electoral prospects and weakened his grip over the Federalist Party. It did not, however, destroy his marriage. The Maria Reynolds scandal and his wife's private discovery of his affair with her sister left Betsy humiliated and heartbroken. Yet she not only stayed with her man but also defended his memory over the fifty years that she outlived him.

Tragically Hamilton died when he was only forty-nine years old and had much still to contribute to America. Aaron Burr, his then political nemesis, challenged him to a duel when he refused to publicly refute criticism of Burr. On July 11, 1804, they met in a meadow near Weehawken, New Jersey, overlooking the Hudson River and New York City. Hamilton came with the intention to fire in the air and thus preserve both honor and life. Burr came with the intention to kill. Burr won.

If the art of American power is one's ability to defend and expand the nation's interests, then no one was a greater master from 1789 to 1800 than Alexander Hamilton. The ends and means of his vision for America are best expressed in the Constitution's preamble: "We the People of the United States, in Order to form a more perfect Union, establish Justice, ensure domestic Tranquility, provide for the common defense, promote the general Welfare, and secure the Blessings of Liberty to ourselves and our Posterity, do ordain and establish this Constitution for the United States of America."

PART 1
Washington, 1789–1793

In framing a system which we wish to last for ages, we should not lose sight of the changes which ages will produce.

JAMES MADISON

The policy of Parliament has been to seize every advantage which our weak and unguarded situation exposes. She has bound us in commercial manacles and very nearly defeated the object of our independence.

JAMES MADISON

In spite of treaties, England is still our enemy.

THOMAS JEFFERSON

1

The Father of His Country

The winner of America's first presidential election under the new Constitution apparently was never in doubt. Each state chose its allotment of electors on January 7, 1789. Just how those electors were chosen varied. The people, or at least those deemed worthy of having a vote, chose electors in five states, while legislators picked them elsewhere. Each state's electors met on February 4, 1789. Then an extraordinary thing happened. The unanimous vote was for George Washington as president. There was no national or regional movement to elect Washington. He was the obvious and only choice, and the electors acted accordingly. Although that spontaneous consensus is astonishing, Washington had "in a certain sense had been acting as President of the United States since 1775."[1]

Once they had chosen the president, each state's electors voted for a vice president. John Adams received a plurality, and ten other candidates split the remainder. As for Congress, each state voted on different dates. The First Congress, which convened in March 1789, included representatives from only the ten states that had ratified the Constitution and held elections in time. Eventually, as the laggards completed the ratification and election processes, they would add their members to the sitting ten senators and fifty-nine representatives.[2]

New York City was the first capital of the United States under the new Constitution and remained so until August 1790, when the entire government packed up and journeyed eighty miles to Philadelphia, where the federal government sat until 1800. The first official capitols were Federal Hall in New York and Independence Hall in Philadelphia.

While Congress had an official residence, the president had to go house hunting. He respectfully declined New York governor George Clinton's offer to lease his opulent home for the duration of the president's tenure in the city. More than generosity lay behind the offer, and more than cost and a desire not to inconvenience the governor was involved in the president's polite refusal. Clinton was among the nation's most powerful, charismatic, and articulate anti-federalists. It definitely would not do for the president to shelter in the governor's shadow.[3]

Eventually the Washingtons moved into a home owned by the merchant and federalist Samuel Osgood, who had previously moved out to accommodate the president of the Confederation. This home served as the executive mansion for eight months, with George and Martha occupying the second floor, his three aides the third floor, and the seven Washington slaves presumably the cellar; the first floor was used for official business. Eventually a much larger residence was found and renovated for the Washingtons and the president's expanding number of officials.

Numerous myths about George Washington have accumulated over the centuries since his presidency, but who was the real man?[4] Unfortunately, many people then and since have taken Washington's reserve and parsimony of tongue to mean that he was not as bright as his more loquacious compatriots. Unlike his cabinet heads, he never attended college, which undoubtedly exacerbated a painful natural shyness. Indeed he may not have had the intellectual depth or expanse of Hamilton, Franklin, or Jefferson, although only a gifted few do at any time. Yet Washington had an exceptional mind, which he was far more comfortable and skilled in expressing with his pen than with his voice. His letters are beautiful compositions of style and substance.

Although he held himself aloof in social or political settings, on the battlefield Washington displayed courage to the point of recklessness. After his baptism of fire, he famously remarked, "I heard the bullets whistle, and believe me there is something charming in the sound."[5] His looming, stoic, six foot four inch presence accounted for a good measure of his charisma. Even though he was fifty-seven when he became president, he was still lean and powerful; he remained at graceful ease in the saddle and on the ballroom floor. Volcanic passions continued to smolder just beneath his stern facade. His occasional eruptions of wrath were well known and feared.

Washington was among the very first genuine American nationalists. He devoted himself to founding and nurturing a republic that not only protected rights but vigorously resolved conflicts, developed the economy, and protected the nation from all threats, foreign and domestic. From his youth, he modeled his character and behavior on Plutarch's *Lives*, which profiled Greek and Roman heroes who personified virtue above all. The ancient hero with whom Washington most closely identified was Cincinnatus, who returned to his plow after serving his country. During its first few decades, the United States had almost continuous need of George Washington.

George Washington's indomitable character shaped his presidency. He ran the country as he had his army. Although few details of government escaped his attention, he never lost sight of the big picture of crucial domestic and foreign challenges confronting the United States. He surrounded himself with capable advisers and listened carefully to their counsel. He had to form a government from scratch because the Constitution makes no mention of how to structure it. The president recommended, and Congress approved, the nation's first four departments. And to fill those posts, Washington tapped Alexander Hamilton to serve as the treasury secretary, John Jay temporarily as the secretary of state (until Thomas Jefferson returned from Paris), Henry Knox as the war secretary, and Edmund Randolph as the attorney general. Ideological and regional diversity seconded experience and intellect in forming those choices.[6]

The president and his men worked tirelessly most of their waking hours. Decisions were reached by debate within his small cabinet and then implemented through the appropriate channels. And although his administration would soon be notorious for the worsening conflict over ideas and egos between Hamilton and Jefferson, the president was firmly in charge.

2

Hamilton versus Jefferson

Alexander Hamilton and Thomas Jefferson were the intellectual and policy titans of Washington's first term. Their differences took a while to emerge and ultimately poisoned their relationship. But at first they worked well together. Although each was well aware of the other's illustrious accomplishments, they did not meet until March 1790, after Jefferson finally arrived to take John Jay's place as secretary of state.

They found common ground on several key issues, including that Britain should be pressed to fulfill its promises under the Treaty of Paris, that Spain should open the Mississippi River to free American passage, and that a campaign against the Ohio Valley Indians should be vigorously pursued. But it became clear that an unbridgeable philosophical chasm split them on questions of the ends and means of American wealth, power, security, culture, and morality.

With his liberal beliefs, experience in war and commerce, and brilliant mind, Alexander Hamilton was the near perfect choice for America's first treasury secretary.[1] He was the leading voice for a muscular, problem-solving, far-sighted national government empowered not just to defend the nation but also to develop finance, commerce, industry, infrastructure, education, high culture, and justice. The trouble was that he had many of the defects of people gifted or cursed with an overabundance of both intellect and passion—he was often impatient, impulsive, imprudent, and confrontational. Over time he seemed to accumulate as many devoted enemies as friends. As treasury secretary he would propose and push a series of programs designed to initiate related financial, commercial, and industrial revolutions for the United States. Had they been completely and competently implemented, America's wealth and power would have developed a generation or more sooner than it did historically.

As the oldest son of a plantation owner in Virginia's piedmont region, Thomas Jefferson certainly enjoyed an easier childhood than Hamilton did.[2] But it was Jefferson's own native genius and ambitions that propelled him into the political elite of not just Virginia but America. He attended the College of William and Mary, passed the bar, served in Virginia's House of Burgesses, was elected to the First and Second Continental Congresses, served a term as Virginia's governor in 1779, returned to Congress in 1781 for six months, and (after a few years at his beloved plantation Monticello) agreed in 1784 to replace Benjamin Franklin as minister to France. He was most famous for expressing the American mind through the Declaration of Independence; he was chosen for that duty because of the renown for the eloquence and profundity of his writings.

Washington's choice of Jefferson as his secretary of state made sense at the time. Jefferson had an outstanding résumé and, as a Virginian, helped balance the administration between southerners and northerners. But while he had ample experience as both a politician and diplomat, his introspection and beliefs complicated his performance. More than an inherent shyness made him a controversial secretary of state when he took over from John Jay on February 22, 1790.

Jefferson was an idealist whose pet theories were often little more than prejudices or sentiments. Although his political outlook was vivid, he never developed it into a coherent system. He shared with Hamilton a devotion to republican principles, but they could not disagree more over how those were best realized. For Jefferson, the individual states rather than the federal government were the proper guardians of liberty. He feared that the strong national government that Hamilton promoted would be nothing more than a disguised tyranny.

Jefferson was also Hamilton's foil over America's economic future and the relationship between government and markets. For Jefferson, the government that governed least governed best. The trouble was that Jefferson was anything but a profound thinker when he addressed economics. Moreover, what he lacked in depth of understanding he more than made up with in the fervor of his beliefs. The foundation of his economics was the sentiment that "those who labor in the earth are the chosen people of God." That notion would have undoubtedly disturbed the slaves chained to the back-breaking drudgery of working his plantation. But Jefferson was immune to such subtleties. When it came to agrarian labor, the vital factor was the amount of land. Americans had "quantities of land to waste as we please. In Europe the object is to make the most of their land, labor being abundant;

here it is to make the most of our labor, land being abundant." He championed Adam Smith's idea that a nation, like an individual, should specialize in what it does best and then trade that for all its other needs. With that logic, he was a zealous free trader: "Our interest will be to throw open the doors of commerce . . . giving perfect freedom to all persons for the vent of whatever they may chose to bring into our ports, and asking the same in theirs." Thus he attacked those "political economists of Europe" who "have established it as a principle that every state should endeavor to manufacture for itself" all its material needs.[3]

When it came to manufacturing, Jefferson went beyond market logic in condemning its development in the United States. Manufacturing was a Faustian bargain in which profit was traded for virtue—"Let us never wish to see our citizens occupied at a work-bench. . . . For the general operations of manufacture, let our workshops remain in Europe." He found virtue in each American family making its own necessities. Farming, however, would remain their central occupation—"we have an immensity of land courting the industry of the husbandman. It is best that our citizens should be employed in its improvement."[4]

Here in the realm of economics is another of those odd clashes between Jefferson's pet theories and his own experience. He spent his life in a realm protected from all but the most voracious of market forces. Even then he failed to make money on any of the many enterprises he nurtured on his plantations, except for his nail-making workshop. That venture most likely would have also lost money had he employed free rather than slave labor.

He did not just hate manufacturing. He condemned the "mobs of great cities [that] add just so much to the support of pure government as sores do to the strength of the human body. It is the manners and spirit of a people which preserve a republic in vigor. A degeneracy in these is a canker which soon eats to the heart of its laws and constitution."[5] His fear of cities and the mobs latent in them is understandable, given the bloodcurdling firsthand accounts he had heard of what atrocities "the people" were committing in the streets and squares of Paris as the French Revolution unfolded. Yet here is another contradiction in his thought and temperament. While he hated mobs, he loved revolutions, including the one erupting beneath his nose when he served in Paris. At times he was less a republican than a wild-eyed anarchist: "The spirit of resistance to government is so valuable that . . . I wish it to be always kept alive. . . . I like a little rebellion now and then. . . . What signifies a few lives lost in a century or two. The tree of liberty must be refreshed from time to time with the blood of patriots and tyrants. It is their natural manure."[6]

Jefferson's philosophy and politics are best understood through his psychology. He was a man tormented by the central contradiction of his life—he at once championed liberty and lived off slavery. He turned a blind eye to the reality that he was a baron in a slavocracy in which a tiny elite amassed nearly all their wealth by exploiting laborers in the harshest possible way.

Instead of resolving that contradiction, he projected onto hated others his own vilest practices. He smeared northern manufacturers, merchants, and bankers as personifying his own vices. He recognized that over time a manufacturing economy would far surpass an agrarian economy in wealth, power, and population. That would be humiliating enough to slaveholders. But the worst nightmare would be if northerners used their political power to abolish slavery. So Jefferson was determined to do anything possible to prevent, or at least delay, that from happening. Tragically, those contradictions between principles and practices in a prominent American policymaker neither began nor ended with him.

Jefferson had an essential ally in his war with Hamilton over policy and principle. James Madison, the Constitution's chief architect and the Federalist Papers' coauthor, wielded an ever less constructive role as the opposition leader in Congress.[7] Historians have dismissed Madison's enduring popular image as a compromiser. He was instead "a revolutionary; his ideological presuppositions, down deep, were immovable; despite all appearances to the contrary, he was one of the most stubborn and willful men of his time. In what to him was fundamental, he was quietly, implacably determined to have his way."[8]

Madison's intellect, learning, and ambition were as keen as his physical stature, voice, and courage were slight. His overbearing father, who was a militia colonel, justice of the peace, and vestryman as well as plantation owner, did contribute something positive to Madison's life in getting him the best available tutors and then sending him off to the College of New Jersey, today's Princeton University.

Madison was a committed revolutionary from the very beginning. He joined the local Committee of Safety in 1774; helped write Virginia's state constitution in 1776; was elected to the Council of State, where he served governors Patrick Henry and Thomas Jefferson; and in 1779 was elected to Congress, where he stayed until 1783. He returned to Virginia's statehouse until 1787, when he was chosen as a delegate to the Constitutional Convention at which he achieved immortality.

During his early career, Madison overcompensated for his timidity on the floors of legislatures, courts, and ballrooms by meticulously building arguments or strategies and feeding them to his bolder and more confident collaborators. He mastered the art of manipulating events from behind the curtain and avoiding any confrontations that would "excite the suspicions of men that he would be in competition with them for anything."[9] But Madison could not obscure all his double-dealings. He acquired a well-deserved reputation for being two-faced, duplicitous, and hypocritical.

No ally was more powerful than his mentor, friend, and ideological soul mate Thomas Jefferson, who was just as bookish, shy, and brilliant. Madison's political successes—and, perhaps more vitally, a romantic success in wooing and wedding Dolley Todd, pretty, vivacious, and seventeen years younger—gradually boosted his confidence. By the Convention he was speaking out, and by the first Congress he was Jefferson's point man on the floor as well as in committee rooms and taverns.

As the author of twenty-nine of the Federalist Papers, Madison advocated a strong central government. Indeed, during the 1780s, the principles and arguments of Madison and Hamilton were often indistinguishable. Then a stunning transformation took place. In the decades ahead, Madison would repudiate ever more of the Constitution's powers and institutions, which he had shaped at the Convention and defended in the Federalist Papers. In doing so he would turn against Hamilton, his once close friend and collaborator. That betrayal of the friendship and principles they once shared would baffle and deeply hurt Hamilton.

Hamilton and those who supported his principles and policies were known as Federalists. Jefferson, Madison, and all others who championed a diametrically opposed notion of American interests, power, and policies called themselves Republicans. Although their respective labels have changed, that vast, unbridgeable chasm has persisted in American politics ever since.[10]

3

Nurturing American Power

The framers had the wisdom to craft a document that would endure for ages and be adapted to the unique challenges of each age. The preamble's list of specific duties of government was worded in a way to be both comprehensive and vague enough so that each generation could interpret them in the light of its own problems and aspirations. To fulfill those duties, the Constitution arms the federal government with a wide enough array of both explicit and implied powers. The most important, however, were perfectly clear—the Constitution was the supreme law of the land, and the government was empowered to enact all "necessary and proper" laws to fulfill its duties. James Madison captured that original intent in a constitution that could be adapted to the demands of future times: "In framing a system which we wish to last for ages, we should not lose sight of the changes which the ages will produce."[1]

Shortly after the new government was inaugurated, Madison spearheaded two reforms that were crucial for consolidating American power. He mobilized a majority to pass the Judiciary Act of 1789, which added layers of district and circuit courts below the Supreme Court. Far more crucially, he headed the committee charged with drawing up a list of rights that would be amended to the Constitution. In all the committee considered over two hundred rights submitted by petitioners. Eventually this list was whittled down and consolidated in seventeen amendments that Madison presented to the House on June 8. The House approved that list and sent it to the Senate, which eventually voted in favor of twelve on September 10. A joint committee dropped two. The House approved

17

the first ten amendments, known as the Bill of Rights, on September 25, and the Senate approved them the following day. Washington signed the bill into law on October 2, 1789, and sent copies to each state assembly for ratification. Virginia became the ratifying state on December 15, 1791.[2]

Those two vital measures aside, thereafter the initiative for nurturing American power lay almost exclusively with the Washington administration. Two inseparable challenges faced the president and his men. They had to consolidate the federal government's power and develop the nation's wealth. The lines blurred between federal and national power, and domestic and foreign policy. Where did one begin and the other end?

No one understood these ambiguities better than Alexander Hamilton.[3] Few Americans then or since had a more long-term view of the nation's development, and to that end the dynamic, changing relationship among American interests, power, and policies. Hamilton very carefully calculated American power and interests, and then just as carefully crafted policies designed to use all appropriate means to advance those interests.

Of course, one key, unchanging national interest is to amass more power, and this animated every Hamilton policy. Hamilton envisioned that one day the United States would "dictate the terms of the connection between the old and new world." It would do so by becoming "the Arbiter of Europe in America; and to be able to incline the balance of European competitions in this part of the world as our interest may dictate."[4]

But that time was far away. Until then, the United States had to keep a discreet international profile. Hubris was a potentially self-destructive path for anyone, especially the weak, and was to be avoided at all costs. With a feeble diplomatic hand, Americans might have to give away more than they received in international negotiations. Such was the fate of second-rate powers. But if the United States nurtured rather than squandered its slowly growing wealth and power, one day it would surpass all others.

Hamilton had been a mercantilist, deficit hawk, and fiscal conservative ever since he began to practice economics as the teenage bookkeeper in a merchant house on St. Croix. The practical lessons he learned from that experience were confirmed by the theories he studied at King's College in New York City. No thinker influenced him more than David Hume, with his pragmatic approach to the relationship between governments and markets or the public and private sectors. Hume argued that government was crucial in helping to create and distribute wealth and that its foremost goal was nurturing the numbers and prosperity of the middle class. To that end, during the dozen years before he became the treasury secretary, Hamilton advocated a strong currency, central bank, taxes, and the eventual elimination of the state and national debts. In doing so he hoped to create a virtuous dynamic economic cycle founded on ever higher growth, investments, incomes, revenues, and savings; ever lower debt, interest rates, and joblessness; and an ever more diverse array of businesses. As the treasury secretary he had the opportunity to realize that vision.

He had a Herculean task before him. The United States was trapped in a vicious economic cycle. The federal and most state governments were bankrupt; the national debt and trade deficits were soaring; ever more money had to be raised within the United States by both the public and private sectors to satisfy foreign creditors; but exporting coins rather than products depressed the economy and government revenues, which further worsened the debt, and so on. Hamilton calculated a total national debt of $79 million, composed of $27 million in congressional debt, $13 million in accumulated interest, $2 million in unliquidated Continental currency, $12 million in foreign debt, and $25 million in state debts.[5]

Among the benefits of trade were revenues for the cash-starved federal government. Tariffs made up virtually all the coins that dropped into the Treasury Department's coffers. Thus, the key to paying off that debt was to expand America's foreign trade and the tariffs skimmed from the volume. Yet the government had to be very careful when it determined tariff rates. Setting tariffs too high would inhibit trade, inflict inflation on American consumers, and actually reduce revenues over the long term. Setting tariffs too low would expose American manufacturers to ruinous competition. Finding the right balance was the key to Hamilton's economic program.

Hamilton faced two related obstacles to fulfilling his vision, one domestic and the other foreign. Jefferson, Madison, and their followers would soon do everything possible to defeat Hamilton's proposals at home. With its vast economic power, Britain was at once the foreign obstacle to and inspiration for Hamilton's policies.

While the United States depended on Britain for most of its trade, Britain's own trade was far more diversified. In 1790 only 17 percent of Britain's exports went to the United States. Although the United States often enjoyed an overall trade surplus, it suffered chronic deficits with Britain. American exports in 1790 were $20,194,794, of which nearly half or $9,246,562 went to Britain. Of $15,388,409 worth of imports, a whopping $13,798,168, or about 90 percent, were British goods. That year, of 90,420 tons of British goods carried by 452 vessels to American ports, 50,979 tons were in 234 British ships and 39,441 tons in 218 American ships. Of 109,521 tons carried by 558 vessels from America to Britain, 64,197 tons went in 312 British ships and 45,234 tons in 246 American ships.[6]

Whitehall made the most of that potentially crushing advantage over the United States, wielding its power to maintain its power. Madison put it well: "The policy of Parliament has been to seize every advantage which our weak and unguarded situation exposed. She has bound us in commercial manacles and nearly defeated the object of our independence."[7]

Hamilton and his fellow Federalists were well aware that America would be devastated in a trade war with Britain and thus sought conciliation rather than confrontation with Whitehall. The Republicans turned a blind eye to such statistics presented by the Federalists and instead insisted that an American embargo would force the British to knuckle under.

Hamilton worked with congressional leaders to carefully devise a tariff bill that would not only raise revenues but also nurture America's shipbuilding industry. His proposed Tonnage Act of 1789 discriminated among ships that dropped anchor in American ports. Those built in and owned by Americans paid a duty of six cents a ton. Those built in the United States but owned by foreigners paid thirty cents a ton. All other ships paid fifty cents a ton.

That was not good enough for James Madison. Although he and Jefferson were ideologically wed to the notion that the government that governs least governs best, they set aside that principle when Britain was involved. Madison upped the mercantilist ante when he introduced a trade bill in the House that would tax not just foreign ships but also the goods they carried.

While Hamilton certainly agreed that one role of government was to tilt the economic playing field in favor of the nation's business, how and when it did so depended on the strategic economic context. For now Hamilton's priority was to arrest and diminish the national debt, which would free up ever more money for investments elsewhere in the economy. But this strategy would demand fine-tuned policies and time. Hamilton feared that Madison's proposal would promote American manufacturers and shipowners at the cost of federal revenues and thus ultimately starve those strategic industries of vital investments over the long term. The result would be to crimp rather than stimulate the creation of American wealth and power. Hamilton explained to Jefferson that for now "my commercial system turns very much on giving a free course to trade, and cultivating good humour with the world. And I feel a particular reluctance to hazard any thing, in the present state of our affairs, which may lead to a commercial warfare with any power."[8]

Madison's bill passed the House. When the Senate took up its own version, Hamilton worked behind the scenes to ensure that it included no discriminatory clauses. His version passed the Senate. A conference was called to reconcile the two versions. The Senate's version prevailed, passed both houses, and was signed by the president into law.

Madison and Hamilton renewed their tug-of-war over trade policy in 1790. This time Madison sought to raise tariffs on British imports and forbid any British ships in American waters unless Britain opened the West Indies to American trade. The House passed his resolution by 32 to 19. Senate Republicans were working on their own version of that resolution. Jefferson put his weight behind that effort by publishing excerpts of letters that he had received that called for retaliation against Britain for its mercantilist policies.

Once again Hamilton urgently explained that if a trade war broke out with Britain, the United States would lose much more than it gained. As if that would not be damaging enough to American interests, there was the chance that a trade war might turn into a shooting war. So the treasury secretary pulled all the strings available with Congress, newspapers, and merchants to ensure that the resolution that eventually passed both houses of Congress was simply a statement of principles and protest stripped of any provocative retaliatory measures.

The next step in Hamilton's economic revolution was articulated in his "Report on Public Credit" and "Report on the Bank of the United States," which he submitted to Congress on December 13 and 14, 1790, respectively. Both reports proposed ways that the federal government could raise revenues and reduce the national debt. The first report called for an excise tax on domestic distilled liquors and higher tariffs on imported liquors. Under his bank proposal, the federal government would assume the debts of the states, combine them into the national debt, and service them with a Bank of the United States that would pay a 6 percent interest rate and collect all national revenues. The bank would be initially capitalized with $10 million, of which $2 million would come from the federal government and the rest as shares from private investors.

Congress eventually approved Hamilton's financial revolution. There was a solid consensus behind the excise tax that passed the House on January 27 and the Senate on February 26, 1791, and took effect in March 1791. His bank proposal sailed through the Senate on January 20 but ran into a wall in the House when debate opened on February 2.

Once again Madison was vitriolic in leading the opposition to Hamilton, and he pulled every legislative lever to kill the bank proposal. His central argument was that if the Constitution did not specially grant the government the power to create such a bank, then it could not be done. With this argument he flip-flopped on the position he had taken in the Federalist Papers. In the forty-fourth essay, he had insisted that the Constitution did indeed empower the government to make "all laws necessary and proper" to fulfill its duties and dismissed the idea that if a power was not specifically listed it did not exist. To rely solely on the enumerated powers would "disarm the government of all real authority." Madison could not have asserted federal power more clearly than when he declared that "no axiom is more clearly established in law or in reason than that wherever the end is required, the means are authorized; whenever a general power to do a thing is given, every particular power necessary for doing it is included."[9]

Hamilton marshaled his own forces. When a vote was held, the bank bill passed by 39 to 20. Washington signed the law on April 25, 1791. The Bank of the United States would be a private business, with the federal government the largest partner. The charter would last twenty years, from 1791 to 1811, and could then be renewed. No other federal bank could be established during that time, although states were free to create their own banks. The bank could not issue notes or borrow money beyond its capitalization. At least 20 percent of the bank's capital had to be held rather than lent. Foreigners were allowed to own shares but could not vote. The director would be annually rotated among the board of directors. The treasury secretary was free to remove federal deposits as he wished and could inspect the books as often as once a week.

Hamilton's jubilance over that triumph soon faded. Madison blocked a bill that would allow the bank to take over the $25 million worth of state debts. Eventually Hamilton was able to persuade Congress to approve his "assumption" plan by a classic backroom political horse trade.[10]

Jefferson hosted the dinner at which the grand swap was alleged to have taken place on the evening of June 28. He describes the background to his ploy:

> I met Hamilton. . . . His look was somber, haggard, and dejected beyond description. Even his dress was uncouth and neglected. He asked to speak with me. . . . He opened the subject of the assumption of the state debts, the necessity of it in the general fiscal arrangement and its indispensable necessity towards a preservation of the union. . . . [I]f he had not credit enough to carry such a measure he could be of no use and was determined to resign. . . . On considering the situation . . . I thought the first step would be to bring Mr. Madison and Col. Hamilton to a friendly discussion of the subject. I immediately wrote each to come and dine with me the next day, mentioning that we should be alone.[11]

The result was a swap of assumption for a $15 million cut in the taxes Virginia owed the United States and a national capital in the south.

Washington signed the Residence Act of 1790 into law on July 16. The law empowered the president to select a ten square mile site for the capital, which would be the federal government's permanent home from 1800. The capital would first switch from New York City to Philadelphia on August 12, 1790, and remain there for a decade. Washington feigned careful study in considering a variety of possible sites before announcing his decision on January 24, 1791. In truth, he had soon settled on the present location. Sadly, he would not live to see the government in the new capital named after himself.

Once the Residence Act passed, Madison was willing to bring the assumption bill to the floor. That bill passed when he and four colleagues withheld their votes. Washington signed the assumption bill into law on July 26.

The First Bank of the United States was an enormous success. Subscriptions were appropriately opened on July 4, 1791. Within one hour eager investors had pocketed all the shares. After the assumption bill passed, Hamilton quickly consolidated the debts and began to impose fiscal sanity upon the federal government. Shorn of their debts, the states were then free to put their own financial houses in order.

Hamilton's financial revolution was not yet complete. In those days a dozen hard currencies and scores of soft currencies, including the nearly worthless Continental dollar and various bank or mercantile drafts, circulated as legal tender through the United States. The value of one currency to another was virtually impossible to determine. As a result, America's economic potential remained grossly stunted.

Hamilton insisted that a national mint be established to produce a national currency with a fixed and substantive value. As sensible as that proposal was, Jefferson and his allies once again protested. The clash between Hamilton and Jefferson over a national currency and mint for the United States dated to 1784. That year, Jefferson had proposed in Congress a dollar composed of 375.6 grains of silver. Hamilton crunched the numbers and pointed out that the weight of this dollar would be greater and the face value would be less than comparable foreign coins, thus giving investors an incentive to buy up American coins. He proposed a dollar with either 371.25 grains of silver or 23.75 grains of pure gold. Rather than admit that Hamilton was right, Jefferson continued to insist that his version be adopted. Yet here again Hamilton bested him. In 1791 Congress passed a law establishing a U.S. mint with a dollar valued on Hamilton's calculations rather than Jefferson's.

Hamilton did not rest on his laurels. It took him over a year to research and compose his "Report on Manufacturing," which he submitted to Congress on December 5, 1791. His plan called for the government to lead an industrial revolution by nurturing the nation's infrastructure and industries, the skeleton and muscle of a modern economy. In doing so he rejected both Thomas Jefferson's notion of an agrarian republic grounded in yeoman farmers and Adam Smith's belief that free markets solved all economic and social problems. Hamilton championed a muscular problem-solving government that would work with the private sector to develop the national economy. He explained that free markets do not exist at the national level. Every market was distorted by public policies and by the power of private investors to gain advantage for themselves through both monopolies or oligopolies and the political marketplace, whether it was called congress, parliament, the "king's will," or something else. He noted that, contrary to free-market theory, most people fear making "a spontaneous transition to new pursuits." Left to a Darwinian marketplace, private investors tended to shy away from investing in roads, canals, ports, schools, and factories that were crucial to economic development. But sound policies could encourage entrepreneurs to risk their money and time through protective tariffs against foreign competitors; tax cuts; infrastructure; societies that gathered, nurtured, and shared information on new technologies; and so on. Without those incentives, the United States would fall ever farther behind Britain, which had been following the same strategy for centuries. Only by forging a dynamic partnership between government and business would America have a chance to catch up to and one day surpass Britain as a global power.[12]

The next step was to translate that report into policy. Hamilton sought to nurture American manufacturers with selective rather than cross-the-board tariffs. The tariff law he proposed in 1792 was a very carefully calibrated document that balanced the needs to nurture manufacturers and raise government revenue. Unfortunately the sophistication of his policy was lost on most politicians. This time the Jeffersonians won by spiking his proposals with majority votes in both houses.

Nonetheless, enough of Hamilton's plans were implemented to spark an economic renaissance for the United States. American exports tripled from $33 million in 1794 to $94 million in 1801. In 1790 American vessels carried less than half of the nation's trade, with 39,441 tons in 218 ships compared to 50,797 tons in 245 British ships. In 1800 they accounted for 82 percent, with 124,015 tons carried in 550 ships compared with 27,144 tons in 77 British ships.[13]

While national power was ultimately grounded in a dynamic economy, Hamilton did not neglect the military. He argued that the United States was in ever more desperate need of a professionally trained, equipped, and led army and navy. As America's territorial and commercial interests expanded, the military had to expand with it. To justify that policy, he pointed not only to the potential threats posed by the British, Spanish, French, and southwestern Indians, but to a chronic undeclared war on the northwest frontier in which American troops had suffered humiliating defeats.[14]

4

Frontier War

Wars between Americans and Indians were as old as the first settlers in the New World.[1] Virtually every such war followed a pattern. Ever more hunters, trappers, traders, and settlers invaded a tribe's territory, decimating the game, stealing the most fertile lands, and debauching the Indians with alcohol. Fighting erupted. Indian warriors launched raids against the settlers along the contested frontier, massacring many inhabitants and bringing loot and captives back to their villages. Those colonies or states that suffered attacks mobilized expeditions that destroyed the enemy villages. With their homes destroyed and short of ammunition and food, the Indians sued for peace. The subsequent treaty promised payments in return for land, and the Indians were driven farther west. Sooner or later the vicious cycle repeated itself.

When Washington became president, the United States faced twin Indian threats in the southwest and northwest. The president was eventually able to secure peace with the southwest tribes, but chronic fighting soon evolved into an all-out war with the northwest tribes. The issue, of course, was land. The northwest tribes were split between those willing and unwilling to cede land to the aggressive Americans. Those willing to cede did so in the treaties of Fort Stanwix in 1784, Fort McIntosh in 1785, Fort Finney in 1786, and Fort Harmar in 1787 and 1789. The final boundary lay along the Cuyahoga River, with its mouth on Lake Erie to its headwaters, then west to the Miami River's headwaters, and then down it to the Ohio River. The tribes retained all lands west and north of that line, leaving the Americans free to own and exploit the rest as they pleased.

As with previous treaties, those of Fort Harmar fell apart because the tribal councils refused to ratify them. Nearly all those headmen and their peoples who had not attended the council insisted that the Ohio and Allegheny Rivers remain the southern and eastern barriers against the relentless Americans. And ever more warriors acted on that assertion by not only attacking those squatters who trespassed on native land, but even settlements in Kentucky and western Pennsylvania. The raids were devastating. By one count, over fifteen hundred settlers were killed between 1783 and 1790. Clearly the United States was involved in an undeclared Indian war that was undeterred and perhaps incited by the peace councils and treaties. The question was how to end the war. Diplomacy had failed miserably. The only choice was to defeat the Indians decisively and impose a peace.[2]

To that end President George Washington authorized a campaign against the northwest tribes in 1790. The plan was for two columns to strike north against them in September. Lt. Col. Josiah Harmar would lead an army of 1,453 men, which included 320 regulars and the rest militia, from Fort Washington, which had been established the previous year in today's downtown Cincinnati on the Ohio River, toward the Maumee River villages, while Maj. John Hamtramck would head a hundred regulars and four hundred militia from Fort Knox at Vincennes toward the upper Wabash River villages.

The campaign was handicapped in crucial ways. The War Department had not been formally established until August 7, 1789. Although, as the artillery commander during the Independence War, Henry Knox had sufficient experience and skills to be the war secretary, Congress failed to appropriate enough money to raise and sustain troops for the war. In September 1790 the army counted only 672 troops, of which 420 were earmarked for the campaign and the rest scattered in small detachments elsewhere, mostly at frontier posts.

Nonetheless, the 1790 campaign was initially successful. Hamtramck's force advanced up the Wabash, burned the village of Vermillion, then safely withdrew to Vincennes. Harmar's marched all the way to the headwaters of the Maumee River and burned the cluster of villages there. Under the leadership of Miami Chief Little Turtle, the warriors from a coalition of tribes across the region gathered, pursued, and caught up to Harmar's army on October 19. They attacked on that day and the next, routed the Americans, killed 75 regulars and 108 militia, and wounded scores more. Harmar holed up with the remnants of his army in Fort Washington.

The United States had suffered a harsh defeat. President Washington replaced Harmar with Arthur St. Clair, the northwest governor, who was restored to his Revolutionary War rank of major general. With Hamilton as his point man,

Washington was able to convince Congress to authorize the raising of another regiment, and he signed that bill into law on March 3, 1791.

The strategy for 1791 was to launch two initial raids by the Kentucky militia to soften up the enemy before St. Clair's campaign inflicted the knockout blow. Charles Scott led the first strike against the Indian villages on the upper Wabash River in June. This was followed by an attack led by James Wilkinson in August. Those raids burned empty villages before safely withdrawing.

It was not until September 17 that St. Clair headed due north with his army of about seven hundred regulars and fifteen hundred militia. They were all deficient in training, equipment, provisions, and competent leaders. Incessant rains slowed the march to a crawl and disintegrated morale. Over a thousand warriors led by Little Turtle and the Shawnee chief Blue Jacket attacked the American camp on November 4. The militia immediately fled, and without support, the regulars soon followed. The Indians, hacking and shooting until they were exhausted, pursued for miles. The result was America's worst disaster in all of its Indian wars— 645 killed and 271 wounded.

Washington relieved St. Clair of the army command but let him remain the northwest governor. In his place, the president tapped Anthony Wayne, who had been a major general during the War for Independence. Washington had mixed feelings about Wayne, whom he described as "open to flattery; vain; easily imposed upon; liable to be drawn into scrapes" and "likely addicted to the bottle."[3] Astonishingly, Wayne was the best of a very bad lot who shared the same deficiencies, but he had one vital difference—Wayne was the only one among them who was a relentless fighter. Indeed, he was known as "Mad Anthony" for his reckless courage as well as his temper. That reputation surely did not guarantee victory. There was a hazy line between aggressiveness and recklessness, and Wayne could shift easily from one to the other. Fortunately, Wayne had matured with age and would prove to be prudent rather than rash on campaign. The president ensured that he had enough money and men to fulfill his mission. On March 5, 1792, he signed into law a bill that raised the army to 5,392 men.

Victory would depend on more than just leadership and numbers. An analysis of the defeats of Harmar and St. Clair revealed that poor organization was as culpable as poor generalship. Companies of regulars and militia were drawn from different garrisons or communities and thrown into the same force without any attempt at training them to work together. The result was chaos at march, camp, and, tragically, battle.

Since 1785 War Secretary Knox had submitted several versions of a new way to organize the army, but Congress voted each down. St. Clair's defeat gave Washington the political capital to finesse congressional opposition. On December 27, 1792, he issued an order that the army would now be called the Legion of the United States. There were two reasons for the new name. First, it handed a political fig leaf to Republicans, who were ideologically opposed to any "standing army" but might be talked into earmarking funds for a fighting force with a name reminiscent of the Roman Republic and its citizen-soldiers. Indeed the number of troops in the American Legion was nearly the same number in one of Caesar's legions. Second, and more importantly, the Legion signified a new approach to warfare.

The Legion was organized along a combined-arms principle whereby each component complemented the others. It was divided into four sublegions of 1,348 men, with each in turn split among two 674-man battalions of four companies each. There would also be a 399-man rifle battalion of four companies, an 83-man troop of light dragoons, and a 63-man artillery company. The Legion appeared to be a revolutionary idea, but it would take years to recruit and train before it could reveal its potential.[4]

As Wayne began building the American Legion, Washington pursued diplomacy with the Indians. The exhilarating victories over Harmar and St. Clair only hardened the Indian position. They sent word that they would talk, but only if the Americans accepted the Ohio and Allegheny Rivers as the boundary. Although Washington had no intention of recognizing that frontier, he agreed to send commissioners to a peace council. He could only hope that Wayne would decisively defeat the Indians and pass a trump card into an absolutely dismal diplomatic hand.

5

British Intrigues

B ritain posed a clear and present danger to the United States, as Whitehall was determined to contain by any means fair or foul the expansion of American wealth and power. Canada's governor, Guy Carleton, Lord Dorchester, received orders to curry favor with the leaders of the trans-Appalachian regions of Kentucky and Tennessee and, ideally, detach them from the United States. He was also instructed to entice Vermont, which had achieved independence during the Revolution both from Britain and from New York, New Hampshire, and Massachusetts, all of which had conflicting claims over the territory.[1] This strategy would largely die after Vermont, Kentucky, and Tennessee became states respectively in 1791, 1792, and 1796.

Dorchester did not just target frontier leaders as possible traitors. He sent Maj. George Beckwith, a trusted staff officer, to New York on five missions to spy on America's national leadership between 1787 and 1790. Beckwith was very good at his work. During each sojourn, he hobnobbed with numerous members of the political and economic elite and picked their brains about the intricacies of American politics and public sentiments. William Johnson, one of his contacts, summed up the different approaches to American policy toward Britain: "There are two parties in our Legislature, both have a view to form a friendly connexion with Great Britain, differing in their ideas as to means; the one is desirous of very moderate measures on our part, and shunning everything that may have the appearance of commercial warfare . . . the other is of the opinion that prompt and spirited resolutions are best calculated to effect this purpose."[2]

Beckwith's most important exchanges were with Alexander Hamilton, who in his reports is given the code name "Number 7" because he was the seventh person that the major had met.[3] Hamilton first received Beckwith in October 1789 and thereafter tried to nurture him as a diplomatic go-between to Dorchester and ultimately Whitehall. But, to Hamilton's disappointment, this initially promising diplomatic back channel proved to be a dead end. Beckwith returned to Canada in late October.

Nonetheless, how Hamilton handled Beckwith reveals the depth of his understanding of American power and interests, as well as his diplomatic skills. He was probably being sincere rather than just diplomatic when at one point he admitted, "I have always preferred a Connexion with you, to that of any other Country. We think in English and have a similarity of prejudices and of predilections." Yet he immediately followed up that flattery by stating, "We wish to form a Commercial Treaty with you to Every Extent to which you may think it for your interest to go." Having presented the prospect of good relations, he then subtlety rattled the nation's saber. He warned that continued British violations of American interests could transform those largely positive feelings into a burning hatred that could led to war. And if that happened, the United States would most likely renew its alliance with France, to the mutual advantage of each. That alliance "may become important to Your West Indian possessions" along with Canada. Having gotten tough with Beckwith, Hamilton then shifted his strategy back from coercion to inducement. He reiterated the desire to be "connected with you by strong ties of Commercial, perhaps of political, friendships."[4]

President Washington, meanwhile, sought to reopen direct talks with Britain, which had died when John Adams gave up after four fruitless years there and returned to the United States in 1788. Washington sent Gouverneur Morris, who was in Paris on private business, to London as his special envoy to resolve three outstanding problems. First, he was to convince the British to fulfill their promise under the 1783 Treaty of Paris to turn over the frontier posts in American territory to the United States and compensate slave owners for the loss of their slaves. He then was to talk the British into signing a treaty that opened their home and imperial markets to American goods and ships. Finally, he was to convince Whitehall to send a minister to the United States.[5]

Morris was officially received on March 29, 1790. During the next half year, he was granted four interviews with Foreign Secretary Francis Osborne, the Duke of Leeds. He eventually left London without having accomplished any of his mission. While the British were certainly obstinate, Morris may well have been more so.[6]

The closest Morris came to a chance of a breakthrough happened on May 20, when he met with Prime Minister William Pitt. Pitt asked Morris if there was some "general ground" on which "some compensation could not be made mutually" and implied that Whitehall might be willing to swap posts for payments on American debts to British merchants. Morris replied, "If I understand you, Mr. Pitt, you wish to make a new treaty instead of complying with the old one." Pitt agreed. Rather than see if he could get a better deal with a new treaty, Morris insisted that Britain adhere to the existing one. Like Hamilton with Beckwith, Morris did not hesitate to allude to the worst conceivable outcome: "The Conduct you have pursued naturally excites Resentment in every American bosom. We do not think it worth while to go to War with you for the Posts, but we know our Rights and will avail ourselves of them when the time and Circumstances may suit."[7]

Morris was emboldened to take a hard line because of a crisis that became public on May 5. Britain and Spain had overlapping claims to the northwestern coast of North America. The possibility of war over that region arose when word reached London that the previous year a Spanish warship had captured two British merchant vessels in Nootka Sound off Vancouver Island. The Pitt government demanded that those ships and crews be released, and backed that stance by noisily mobilizing the British fleet for attacks on vulnerable strategic sites of Spain's empire. The crisis eventually dissolved after July 24, when Madrid bowed to British power and promised to release the ships and crews. But until then Morris was confident that Whitehall "will give us a good Price for our Neutrality, and Spain I think will do so too, this appears to be a favorable Moment for treating with that Court about the Mississippi."[8]

Pitt was impervious to Morris's saber rattling. He calmly explained that the posts would be rendered only if the Americans made good on their prewar debts to British merchants, let British fur traders operate in American territory, and established an inviolable Indian homeland as a buffer between the American settlements and Canada.

Morris rejected those demands. Certainly the notions of setting up an Indian homeland and letting British traders roam free were nonnegotiable. However, he may have overplayed a weak hand by demanding that Britain adhere to the treaty without acknowledging America's own violations. He also appears to have competed with his British counterparts in who could act more disdainful toward the other. He further annoyed the Pitt government by associating with opposition leader Charles James Fox. As a result, he got nothing other than an agreement to exchange ministers.[9]

Nonetheless, Morris's not so veiled warning to Pitt atop Hamilton's warning to Beckwith the previous year did make an impact. The nightmare scenario in both

London and Quebec was an American alliance with Spain and France against Britain, first to capture the forts on American territory and then to invade Canada itself.

Dorchester received alarming new instructions from William Wyndham, Lord Grenville, the foreign secretary. The nation teetered at war's brink over the Nootka Sound crisis. The governor at the very least had to secure American neutrality and ideally an alliance with Britain against Spain. Dorchester sent word to his frontier commanders to discourage the Indians from warring against the Americans. In June 1790 he dispatched Beckwith back to New York to gather more intelligence and tell Hamilton that it was in American interests to ally with Britain.[10]

Beckwith's suggestion astonished Hamilton when they met on July 8. He hurried to Washington and explained the nature of their talks. The president called together his secretaries, Vice President John Adams, and Supreme Court Justice John Jay for the first of a half-dozen meetings throughout July and August to craft the proper policy.[11]

Beckwith's message was swiftly dismissed. The president had recently received word from Morris that the British would not change their policy toward the United States, so he naturally assumed that Beckwith had exceeded his orders. The concern then arose that, if a war erupted, Britain would demand permission to cross American territory and attack Spain's settlements down the Mississippi Valley. If so, how should the administration respond? The United States had no power in the Ohio Valley to resist an advance. So what transit fee should Britain be asked to pay? And what if, in the worst scenario, Britain spurned any concessions to the United States and conquered the Louisiana and Florida territories? Then, as Jefferson put it to Washington, Britain "will encircle us completely by these possessions on our landboard, and her fleets on our seaboard."[12] Hamilton and Jefferson naturally differed in how they assessed the threat and possible solutions.

Hamilton pointed out that America's diplomatic hand was weak because its military was weak. The Washington administration would only suffer a humiliating rebuff if it insisted on concessions should Britain demand to cross American territory. Nonetheless, a war between Britain and Spain could serve American interests. Rather than try to fight with one against the other, it was in America's interest to trade neutrality to both, with Spain accepting American navigation on the Mississippi River and Britain withdrawing from American territory.[13]

Jefferson argued that the best response would be no response at all. That would at least spare the United States the shame of having the British brutally ignore a firm refusal. At best, the ambiguity of the silence might deter the British from marching. If Whitehall offered concessions, America's minimal demands should be Britain's surrender of the forts, the setting of a fair amount for the debt owned by Americans, and opening of the West Indies to American trade. But Jefferson reckoned it unlikely that Britain would ever concede one let alone all three of those demands. And should Britain violate American territory, the United States "must enter immediately into the war, or pocket the insult in the face of the world; and one insult pocketed soon produces another." Ideally the United States would go to war with allies like Spain and France: the United States "ought to make ourselves parties in the general war expected to take place, should this be the only means of preventing the calamity."[14]

Washington forged a consensus on the similar positions of Hamilton and Jefferson. Clearly a war between America's two neighbors offered both potential rewards and dangers. Each would seek American neutrality and perhaps an outright alliance. While the United States had to avoid getting entangled in that war at all costs, it should indeed ask for a list of concessions from each in return for neutrality. Yet Washington acknowledged the risks in that diplomatic balancing act. If the United States appeared to be anything other than scrupulously neutral, it could risk suffering retaliation from the aggrieved. So the Americans would play off Britain and Spain against each other by explaining that while the United States preferred neutrality, it would certainly consider allying with the other side if concessions were not made to American interests.

American ministers in London, Madrid, and Paris would initiate the policy. Jefferson instructed Morris to convey to Whitehall the United States' desire for neutrality along with a thinly veiled threat that "we will be so, if they will execute the treaty fairly, and attempt no conquests adjoining us." Meanwhile, Col. David Humphreys, one of Washington's most trusted former aides, was dispatched with the same message to Madrid, where he would work with Chargé d'Affaires William Carmichael. Finally, William Short, the American chargé d'affaires in Paris, asked Lafayette to work on Spain's minister there.[15]

Washington asked Hamilton to see what kind of understanding he might forge with Beckwith to advance American interests. As usual, Hamilton's strategy mixed flattery, enticements, and veiled threats.[16] He began by recounting all that their nations shared:

> I have already explained my opinions very fully on the mutual advantages that must result to the two countries from an approximation in commercial matters. In the first instance foreign nations in commerce are guided solely by their respective interests in whatever concerns their intercourse.

Between you and us there are other circumstances; originally one people, we have a similarity of tastes, of language, and general manners. You have a great commercial capital and an immense trade. We have comparatively no commercial capital, and are an agricultural people, but we are a rising country, shall be great consumers, have a preference for your manufactures, and are in the way of paying for them.

After having fed Beckwith that carrot, he then brandished the stick: "You have considerable American and West India possessions. Our friendship or enmity may soon become important with respect to their security." He then reassured Beckwith that if the British evacuated the posts, then they need not fear any threat from the United States because "we have no desire to possess anything northward of our present boundaries."

Hamilton then returned to the theme of mutual interests, this time against Spain. He declared, "The navigation of the Mississippi we must have and shortly. We must be able to secure it by having a post at the mouth of the river, either at New Orleans or somewhere near it. . . . We consider ourselves perfectly at liberty to act with respect to Spain in any way most conducive to our interests, even to the going to war with that power, if we shall think it advisable to join you."

He ended with yet another carefully crafted mix of a subtle threat and an equally subtle inducement: "You know we have two parties with us. There are gentlemen who think we ought to be connected with France. . . . There are others who are at least as numerous and influential, who evidently prefer an English connection." Thus "it would be an act of wisdom in the ministers of Great Britain to attach and connect the States upon political as well as commercial considerations."

Fortunately, the crisis passed without a war. The scare was positive in the sense that it forced the president and his advisers to vigorously discuss America's foreign policy ends and means. And Whitehall did grant one concession—it would send an official minister to the United States.

Britain's first minister to the United States reached Philadelphia on October 20, 1791. George Hammond was young, a mere twenty-eight years old, bright, energetic, and determined to assert his country's interests against the upstart nation.[17] His instructions were straightforward. While Britain would not be bound by a trade treaty with the United States, it would condescend to treat American products to most favored nation status. As for the posts, Britain would retain them until America's debtors paid up. Those instructions were based on Charles Jenkinson, Lord Hawkesbury's "Report on the American Commerce of 1791." Hawkesbury summed up the general view that the posts are of great service in securing the fidelity and attachment of the Indians, and as they afford to Great Britain the means of commanding the navigation of the Great Lakes and the communication of the said Lakes with the River St. Lawrence, they are certainly of great importance to the security of Canada, and . . . should remain in His Majesty's possession if the conduct of the United States should continue to justify this measure on the part of Great Britain.[18]

Jefferson deliberately let Hammond cool his heels for over a month before receiving him and was all business when he finally had the minister ushered in. He wanted written answers to two key questions—the future of the posts and trade. He then abruptly dismissed the minister. For now their official communications would be solely in writing.

Over the next several weeks Jefferson and Hammond exchanged letters that restated each side's already well-known positions but did nothing that even began to resolve any pressing issue. His Majesty would settle the trade and post disputes if the United States fulfilled its duties under the 1783 treaty. To that end the minister was fully empowered to enter negotiations. Jefferson did not mince his words in criticizing an array of British transgressions, especially the confiscation of slaves during the war and the illegal occupation of American territory thereafter.[19]

Hamilton soon established his own relations with Hammond. While he was just as unyielding in presenting America's positions, he was genial in doing so and at least gave the impression of flexibility and compromise. He politely declined a British offer to mediate an end to the war between the United States and the northwest Indians. He readily recognized Britain's prewar claims against American debtors but pressed Hammond to accept British liability for the destruction of property and confiscation of slaves during the war. But his priority was getting Whitehall to open markets in Britain and the West Indies to American goods and ships. The one-time exchange of money across the Atlantic to settle the debt and damage issues would pretty much be a wash. Open markets, however, would be a perennial source of growing wealth for the United States.[20]

In all Hamilton sought to play Hammond with a classic good cop–bad cop routine. Having shown the British minister a different style, if not substance, in presenting America's position and hinting at grounds for compromise, he then temporarily left the diplomatic field solely to Jefferson. However, rather than subtly playing off Hamilton's diplomatic riffs, the secretary of state continued to play his own tune. He spent much of early 1792 preparing a point-by-point attack on each British position and launched that assault on May 29. The logic and evidence that Jefferson mustered were nearly flawless but more suited for a courtroom than a diplomatic table. Jefferson did soften his intellectual barrage by asking Hammond to dine with him so "we might consider the matter together in a friendly way."[21] Thereafter they met to discuss the issues.

Yet, despite the newfound pleasantries, neither side would yield. And so the negotiations, such as they were, deadlocked. It would be another two years before a deal was struck—one so seemingly bad for most American interests that the president and his men would do everything conceivable to hide the details from Congress and the public for as long as possible.

Another crisis broke out between Britain and Spain in 1792. Hamilton now called for an alliance with Britain that would let the United States launch a campaign down the Mississippi Valley to capture Spain's territory east of that river. Washington and his other advisers rejected the proposal as unrealistic. The army had suffered two humiliating and devastating defeats by the Indians in the Northwest Territory. If the United States could not crush those tribes, how could it possibly muster enough troops and leadership to defeat Spain? The logic was irrefutable. Luckily, the United States once again was spared the choice when the British and Spanish defused the crisis.

Then came word that the British were stirring the Indians against the American frontier. The previous year, on February 10, 1791, a delegation of western Indians representing a dozen tribes met with Dorchester and asked the British to war openly with them against the Americans. Dorchester politely declined the request.

That policy changed after Col. John Simcoe was named the first governor of Upper Canada when that province was designated on May 16, 1791. He hated America and Americans. During the Independence War, he had led the Queen's Rangers, a regiment composed of American loyalists, against the rebels. Now he was determined to use his power to contain American expansion. Simcoe worked closely with Sir John Johnson, the Indian superintendent, and Alexander McKee, the deputy Indian superintendent at Detroit, to ensure that the northwest tribes secretly received all the munitions and encouragement they needed to wage war against the United States.

6

Spanish Stonewalling

Spain remained as determined as Britain to contain the United States. Louisiana governor Francisco Luis Héctor de Carondelet explained the nature of the American threat: "This . . . restless population, continually forcing the Indian nations backwards upon us, is attempting to get possession of all the vast continent. . . . If they obtain their purpose, their ambitions will not be limited to this part of the Mississippi. . . . Their method of spreading themselves and their policy are so much to be feared . . . as are their arms."[1]

Thomas Jefferson wanted to break the diplomatic logjam with Madrid. In a letter to George Washington on March 23, 1790, he advised that William Carmichael, the chargé d'affaires, be instructed to revive talks with the Spanish over the Mississippi, the border, and trade. Washington agreed. Unfortunately, the Spanish gave Carmichael a diplomatic brush-off.[2]

When word of the Nootka Sound crisis reached New York in July 1790, Jefferson recognized that if the United States skillfully played off Spain and Britain, it could advance its interests with both. To Madrid, Jefferson sent Col. David Humphreys to work with Carmichael to reopen talks over navigation and the border. The secretary of state also penned instructions to William Short in Paris to enlist Lafayette as the point man in pressuring Spain's minister there. In return, the United States would promise to be neutral. Jefferson explained his strategy: "Nothing short of actual rupture is omitted. The nail will be driven as far as it will go peaceably."[3]

That diplomatic offensive soon ran smack into Spanish intransigence. In Madrid, Foreign Minister Floridablanca once again dismissed the American position of

Carmichael, now backed by Humphreys. In Paris, Lafayette as always was eager to help but was unable to interest the Spanish minister, who lacked instructions and was inundated with more pressing issues.

The only encouraging word came from Philadelphia, where Diego de Gardoqui had turned over Spain's mission to his aides, José de Jáudenes y Nebot and José Ignacio de Viar, and returned to Madrid. Jáudenes and Viar assured Jefferson in December 1791 that Floridablanca was interested in resuming talks. What prompted that turnabout? The Spanish were sobered by the Nootka Sound crisis and what appeared to be a budding rapprochement between the United States and Britain. The promise of talks was a sensible bone to toss to the Americans.

Jefferson eagerly seized that chance. Having not heard anything from Carmichael and with Humphreys now serving in Lisbon, he got Washington's approval to send William Short to Madrid to shake things up. Jefferson had little confidence in Carmichael but could rest easier if Short, his former aide, was on the ground.

A key bargaining chip in any talks with Madrid was America's debt to Spain. As treasury secretary, Hamilton was in charge of the financial side of American diplomacy. In 1792 he instructed Carmichael to inform the Spanish government of America's intention to pay off its loan from Spain, which he calculated at $174,011, including an interest of 5 percent from the date the loan was issued; that bill reached $266,033.62 by the time it was finally paid on August 11, 1793, in Madrid. A different debt of $74,087, including interest, would be paid in Philadelphia in 1794.[4]

Yet another conflict with Spain was over the loyalties of the southwest Indians. These tribes were skilled at manipulating the tug-of-war over their allegiances between the United States and Spain. President Washington invited Creek chief Alexander McGillivray and a delegation of a half-dozen subchiefs to New York in 1790. In a treaty signed on August 7, the Creeks recognized the sovereignty of the United States in return for a guarantee of their lands and $1,500 worth of goods. McGillivray was named an honorary general in the U.S. army and received an annual salary of $1,800. The subchiefs each received an annual stipend of $100. McGillivray continued to receive $600 annually from Spain for acting as an envoy to the Creek people, and in 1792 he signed a treaty with Spain that repudiated the treaty with the United States. The Cherokees signed a similar treaty with the United States in 1791; for an annuity of $1,500, they also become the wards of the United States.[5]

Madrid, like London, tried to entice the westerners in Kentucky and Tennessee to switch sides. For years, Madrid had made it difficult for western merchants to float their goods down the Mississippi River and sell them in Louisiana markets. By doing so, the hope was that those isolated and neglected settlements would break away from the United States and join the Spanish empire. But that dream died when Kentucky became a state in June 1792.

Thus Madrid shifted its policy to encouraging Americans to immigrate to Louisiana and the Floridas in return for converting to Catholicism and making a loyalty oath to the Spanish crown. Thomas Jefferson reacted with glee when he heard about that policy: "I wish a hundred thousand of our inhabitants would accept the invitation. It will be the means of delivering to us peaceably, what may otherwise cost us a war. In the meantime we may complain of this seduction of our inhabitants just enough to make [the Spanish] believe we think it is a very wise policy for them, & confirm them in it."[6]

7

America and the French Revolution

Americans were essentially united in cheering the French Revolution as it unfolded from May through August 26, 1789, when the National Assembly issued the Declaration of the Rights of Man, which so clearly echoed the principles of the Declaration of Independence. Americans took great pride that the French, whose aid was crucial to winning the Independence War, were now inspired by America's example to create their own republic.[1]

No one exceeded Thomas Jefferson's enthusiasm for the French Revolution. He had set sail to the United States in October 1789, when France's progress toward republicanism was exhilarating and the outbreaks of violence were relatively mild and sporadic. He would cling to that image of the French Revolution no matter how much news reached America's shores of ever-worsening atrocities and authoritarianism. Jefferson made a revealing reply to William Short's reports of the unfolding horrors in Paris: "The tone of your letters had for some time given me pain on account of the extreme warmth with which they censured the proceedings of the Jacobins of France." Jefferson then proceeded to justify violence if it championed liberty.[2]

Jefferson's replacement as minister was not quite as sanguine. Gouverneur Morris originally went to Paris in February 1789 to press American claims against French importers. He has left us an entertaining and insightful diary of his experiences there. Like countless other men, he fell in love with all the charms of French culture and women, and stayed on after his mission was done. In 1791 he was delighted to accept Washington's request that he fill the post of minister, which had been vacant since Jefferson's departure.[3]

41

While Morris loved Paris, he was appalled by the revolution's maelstrom of worsening violence, destruction, and terror. He illy disguised his loathing for the radical Jacobins, and they despised him just as heartily. They protested when they learned that Morris had been appointed the minister rather than William Short, the astute and sympathetic chargé d'affaires, who would first be sent to Madrid and then The Hague.

Morris presented his credentials to Foreign Minister Charles-François Dumouriez in May and was ushered before King Louis XVI on June 3, 1792. His most important official duty was to oversee the repayment of America's debt to France, but behind the scenes, he did whatever he could to bolster the royalists and moderates against the Jacobins. His greatest intrigue was to assist the attempt to spirit Louis XVI and his family secretly out of France. That plot died at Varennes, just a few miles from the border, when the national guard captured the royal family and brought them back to Paris. He was successful in helping Lafayette, one of the American Revolution's greatest heroes, to escape from France. Unfortunately, rather than welcome him as a key defector, the Austrians imprisoned him. News of Lafayette's fate upset most Americans, none more than Washington, who looked upon him as a son. He instructed Morris and Short to do what they could to secure his release. Morris sent Lafayette money to sustain himself in prison.[4]

The American Revolution had inspired many of France's revolutionaries. After they took power, they sought closer ties with the United States and were disappointed when the Americans did not immediately and enthusiastically embrace their new "sister republic." The National Assembly voted to place the Stars and Stripes in that chamber and would later be disappointed to learn that neither house of Congress had reciprocated by displaying the Tricolor.

As ever-more crowned heads of Europe limited or outright ended their realms' trade with the increasingly radical regime in Paris, the French sought to make up their losses by expanding their trade with the United States. On June 2, 1791, the National Assembly voted unanimously to negotiate a new treaty with the United States and dispatched Jean Baptiste de Ternant to ask for talks to begin. Shortly after reaching Philadelphia in August, Ternant met Jefferson and asked him to send a special envoy to Paris for negotiations.

Jefferson was amenable to the notion of a more liberal trade treaty but wanted talks to be held in Philadelphia rather than Paris. Neither Jefferson nor Ternant would yield on their preference. After two months of stalemate, Hamilton met with Ternant in October 1791, when the secretary of state was away. While he agreed to a treaty and negotiations in Paris, he wanted higher tariffs than Jefferson had considered. Nothing came of that initiative either. In April 1793 Jefferson tried to revive the issue by explaining to Ternant that the United States desired a trade treaty with France based on equal access to each other's markets and low tariff rates. But, the word that France had declared war on Britain scuttled any chance of talks at that time.[5]

From 1789 to 1794, each stage of France's revolution was more brutal than the last. American views of that revolution split wider as ever-more gruesome reports of rampaging mobs and mass murders reached the United States. While the Republicans continued to celebrate the French Revolution, the Federalists became ever-more skeptical and fearful. Two books, Edmund Burke's *Reflections on the French Revolution* and Thomas Paine's impassioned rebuttal, *The Rights of Man*, expressed the philosophical differences between Federalists and Republicans toward not only the French Revolution but politics in general; the former emphasized moderation, stability, and reform, while the latter espoused a radical egalitarianism.

8

The Widening National Rift

While the Federalist and Republican Parties would take several years to coalesce, the divisions were evident as soon as the First Congress convened on March 4, 1789. Voting records indicate that during his first term, Washington enjoyed the luxury of Federalist congressional majorities. During the First Congress, his allies numbered 18 to 8 in the Senate and 37 to 28 in the House. During the Second Congress, which opened on October 24, 1791, Washington's edge narrowed to 16 to 13 in the Senate and 39 to 30 in the House.[1]

Jefferson was a loyal member of Washington's administration for his first year as secretary of state. He would support a policy after it was adopted even if he disagreed with it. But he was becoming ever more frustrated with Hamilton's intellectual and political triumphs over him. Rather than adjust his views, he fought back all the harder, although secretly behind the scenes rather than man to man.

The turning point came when Hamilton's bank bill became law in February 1791. Thereafter Jefferson worked assiduously and covertly through his fellow anti-Federalists in Congress and the newspapers to resist virtually every measure promoted by Hamilton and the Federalists. He and Madison also began to mobilize the coalition of politicians and newspaper editors who had consistently opposed the Washington administration's agenda into the Republican Party.

The first step was to seek a newspaper editor who could trumpet their ideas, publish their essays under pseudonyms, and lambaste the Federalists. They found their man in Philip Freneau.[2] He was a Princeton graduate, poet, and schoolteacher

44

before he sallied forth on a privateer during the Revolution. He was caught and spent six weeks in a British prison ship before being released. He was lucky both for being freed so soon and having survived at all—perhaps as many as eight thousand Americans died in prison ships during the war. But the brief horrors that Freneau endured left him with a lifelong hatred of the British empire. He first got into the newspaper business in 1781 as the editor of the *Freeman's Journal* of Philadelphia, where he wielded his typeset to skewer the high and mighty with venomous prose. In 1790 he took his literary pit dog skills to New York, where he edited the *Daily Advertiser*, the city's leading anti-Federalist newspaper.

Jefferson and Madison were so impressed that they resolved to set up Freneau with his own newspaper, which would broadcast their political agenda. The first step was for Jefferson to hire Freneau as a clerk at the State Department on February 28, 1791, two days after Hamilton's bank bill passed Congress. Freneau's apprenticeship had much more to do with nurturing political intrigues than foreign policy. Jefferson and Madison coordinated a subscription drive. The first edition of Freneau's *National Gazette* appeared in October 1791.[3]

Jefferson and Madison followed up that crucial step with a "botanizing tour" of upper New York and New England from May 17 to June 19, 1791. The specimens they were actually after were powerful political allies, such as George Clinton, Aaron Burr, and Robert Livingston. A key element of their mission was to cultivate allies in the Federalist stronghold of New England. They wanted their party not only active but dominant in every state.

During the summer of 1791, the Republican Party, which remained secret so as not to offend the prevailing prejudice against "factions," launched a systematic full-scale attack against Federalists across the country. The focal point of their onslaught was Hamilton, whom they demonized as the embodiment of all political and moral evils. By pillorying Hamilton, the Republicans indirectly attacked George Washington, whom Jefferson and Madison sadly believed had betrayed their class and state.

The Federalists were as much bewildered as angered by the ferocity of the attacks. At one point Thomas Jefferson expressed his frustration to John Adams, noting that "you and I differ in our ideas of the best form of government." This surprised Adams, who was unaware that they had any differences. He replied, "I know not what your idea is of the best form of government. You and I have never had a serious conversation together that I can recollect concerning the nature of Government. The very transient hints that have passed between us have been jocular and superficial, without ever coming to any explanation." Adams then went on to dismiss the calumnies his enemies circulated against him that he favored a monarchy and aristocracy.[4] But Jefferson, along with Madison and their swelling party, preferred slander to the inconvenient truth.

After having spent nearly a year covertly laying the groundwork, Jefferson and Madison decided in January 1792 that the time had come to unveil the Republican Party. The impetus was Hamilton's latest economic plan, this one on manufacturing. It was the last straw for the Jeffersonians.

Madison issued a call to arms on January 23, 1792. In the first of eighteen essays that appeared over the next year, he justified parties as a necessary evil and then articulated what would be the Republican Party platform. As in the Federalist Papers, in which he argued that liberty could be preserved only by having a government in which interests countered interests, he now championed political parties with the same logic. In doing so, he abandoned a key value. In the Federalist Papers, he had condemned "factions" as poisonous to a republic. Now he was mobilizing a faction dedicated to interests and values that were diametrically opposed to those he had formerly championed.[5]

The Federalists took longer to organize as a party than the Republicans. For several years after the Constitution was ratified, the Federalists had more a philosophical outlook than an organization. They saw no need to set up a formal party since they already dominated government and were morally opposed to "faction." Hamilton deeply lamented the emergence of the Republicans, noting that "the spirit of Party has grown to maturity sooner in this country than perhaps was to have been counted upon."[6]

Yet, as the attacks on him and other Federalists grew more vicious, Hamilton realized that political survival depended on forming his own party with which to fight back. He found a foil to Freneau in John Fenno and his *Gazette of the United States*, which was also located in Philadelphia. A newspaper war erupted between the *National Gazette* and the *Gazette of the United States* in 1792 and burned for years thereafter. Like Jefferson and Madison, Hamilton used his newspaper ally as a conduit for anonymous essays that blasted the other side. In his first essay, which appeared on August 4, 1792, he outed Jefferson as "the declared opponent of almost all the important measures which had been devised by the government" even though he was "the head of a principal department of the Government." A letter from Washington to Hamilton on July 29, which detailed the harsh criticisms that Jefferson had privately shared with the president over the previous months, provoked that first essay.[7]

Hamilton's essays triggered another round of unfounded charges by the Republicans and then the latest spirited defense by Hamilton. The battle intensified in December 1792 when the administration introduced a bill that would divert $2 million from servicing the debt to France to repay a loan made by the government for stock in the Bank of the United States. In Congress, Virginia representative William Giles had become the Republicans' new point man. Giles responded to the money bill by introducing on January 23, 1793, five resolutions that demanded that all the government's financial account books be opened to the public, at the same time implying that enormous corruption was taking place behind closed doors. Hamilton promptly complied to counter the allegations. Although this particular Republican attack was diluted, the false accusations served only to swell the bitterness between the parties.

These worsening political divisions clouded the end of George Washington's first four years in office, a term that was otherwise highly successful. The president and his men had consolidated the new government's powers and laid the institutional and policy foundations for the nation's economic development. Yet the president despaired at the worsening animosities between Jefferson and Hamilton. In August 1792 he decried the "internal dissensions . . . harrowing and tearing our vitals" and pleaded with both men to display "mutual forbearances, and . . . yieldings on all sides."[8] Tragically but inevitably, these divisions and animosities would only worsen and clip the wings of a fledgling American power.

PART 2

Washington, 1793–1797

*If we desire to avoid insult, we must be able to repel it. If we desire to
secure peace . . . it must be known that we are at all times ready for war.*

GEORGE WASHINGTON

Nature has done everything for us; Government everything against us.

JOHN BRECKINRIDGE

*Self-preservation is the first duty of a nation. Good faith does not
require that the United States should put in jeopardy
their essential interests.*

ALEXANDER HAMILTON

We are being invited to engage in a contest of self-denial. For what?

FISHER AMES

*The Great Rule of Conduct for us, in regard to foreign nations,
is in extending our commercial relations to have with them
as little political connection as possible.*

GEORGE WASHINGTON

9

The Second Term Team

Once again no one opposed George Washington for the presidency or voted against him in the Electoral College, although three delegates withheld their votes. Nonetheless, his political honeymoon had long since passed. The worsening animosities between the Republicans and Federalists both reflected and shaped seemingly irreconcilable differences in American politics. The Third Congress, which convened on December 2, 1793, was split, with the Federalists having a slight edge of 16 to 14 in the Senate and the Republicans 54 to 51 in the House. The parties would widen their respective majorities in the Fourth Congress, which opened on December 7, 1795, with the Federalists enjoying a 21 to 11 lead in the Senate and the Republicans 59 to 47 in the House. The Republican stronghold in the House would stymie or dilute many of Washington's initiatives.[1]

The ever-more-bitter partisanship turned the administration into a pressure cooker. Washington's original cabinet began to break up as one secretary after another resigned, exhausted by the endless work and criticism.

Jefferson, the first to resign, bowed out on January 1, 1794. The president replaced him as secretary of state with Edmund Randolph, a prominent Virginia lawyer who interrupted his practice to serve as a delegate to Congress from 1779 to 1782, as Virginia's governor from 1786 to 1788, and as America's first attorney general from 1789 to 1794. He was a fervent Republican. Jefferson was instrumental in talking Washington into appointing Randolph as his successor. His most notable deficiency was a void of expertise in foreign affairs.

Next to go was Secretary of War Henry Knox, who resigned on December 31, 1794. The president replaced him with Timothy Pickering, a thoroughly undistinguished and inappropriate choice. Pickering had been competent enough as the army's adjutant general from 1777 to 1783 and as postmaster general since 1791, and had negotiated the Treaty of Canandaigua with the Iroquois. But he had nothing else to recommend him.

Alexander Hamilton, the treasury secretary, departed the cabinet to resume his New York law practice on January 31, 1795. To replace him, Washington tapped Oliver Wolcott Jr., who had been the Treasury's comptroller and essentially Hamilton's understudy since 1789. Wolcott was bright and competent enough as an administrator, but he lacked Hamilton's understanding of the dynamic relationship between wealth and power and the skills to nurture more of both.

Edmund Randolph did not last long as secretary of state. A scandal forced his resignation on August 12, 1795. Timothy Pickering was the president's fourth choice to follow Randolph as secretary of state. He then tapped James McHenry to fill the post of war secretary vacated by Pickering. McHenry, a prominent Baltimore physician and merchant, was the oddest choice of all since he had no military experience.

Of all those who departed, none was more bitter than Thomas Jefferson. Hamilton had bested him in nearly every intellectual and political contest between them. To Washington, Jefferson wrote, "I will not suffer my retirement to be clouded by the slanders of a man whose history, from the moment at which history stooped to notice him, is a tissue of machinations against the liberty of the country which has not only received and given him bread, but heaped its honors on his head."[2] Jefferson's departure relieved some of the backbiting within the administration, but now that he was a private citizen, Jefferson could openly assail the Federalist agenda.

1 0

The Genêt Wild Card

The French Revolution topped the list of divisive issues as Washington's second term opened. Initially, most Americans had rejoiced at word of France's transformation from an absolute into a constitutional monarchy during the long summer of 1789.[1] But that enthusiasm cooled over the following years as stories of dictatorship, fanaticism, and mass atrocities reached America's shores. Federalist skepticism toward the French Revolution turned to an ever-fiercer antipathy, while the more thoughtful Republicans grew wary. Then came the outbreak of war in Europe in April 1792.

Technically, the United States bore no military duty to aid France after its National Assembly declared war against Austria and Prussia on April 20, in response to months of ever more provocative counterrevolutionary acts by Vienna and Berlin. The 1778 alliance treaty between the United States and France was defensive. Most Americans were undoubtedly relieved when their flawed sister republic repelled an invasion at Valmy on September 20, 1792, then launched counteroffensives into the Low Countries and along the Rhine. They compared those successes with America's victories against the British in 1775, which culminated with the invasion of Canada.

Then came a succession of ever more radical steps by the revolutionaries. Word arrived that on November 19, 1792, Paris had declared a revolution without borders. By making monarchy the enemy, the French alienated every crowned leader across Europe. Even more disturbing was news of the execution of Louis XVI on January 21, 1793, followed by the war declarations against Britain and Holland on

February 1 and Spain on March 23. As the war spread across Europe, the Caribbean, and the seas in between, Americans naturally feared getting dragged into the conflagration. This provoked acrimonious debate between the Federalists and Republicans over how France's ever more radical revolution would affect American interests and how the United States should respond.

Those developments clearly weakened the power of the United States. With Britain and Spain now allied against a common enemy, the Americans could no longer play one against the other. Indeed, any American threat against one risked bringing the wrath of both down upon the United States. While Britain's army was not powerful enough to successfully invade France, its navy soon began systematically sweeping the seas of French war and merchant ships and, beginning June 8, 1793, any neutral vessels sailing to French ports.

France responded by opening its home and colonial ports alike to whoever was willing to risk the voyage. The owners of hundreds of American vessels eagerly sought profits in those new markets. But no matter where American merchants tried to peddle or purchase goods, they faced a cruel dilemma—to trade with one nation meant being vulnerable to seizure by its enemies. And as the captures of American ships soared, the pressure mounted on the Washington administration to stop the attacks.

Amid these worsening anxieties Edmond-Charles Genêt and the French frigate *Embuscade* reached Charleston on April 8, 1793. As France's new minister to the United States, Genêt's central mission was to enlist the support of the American government and people behind the cause of France's revolution and wars of liberation. Ideally that would mean reviving the moribund 1778 alliance, although most of France's leaders thought that was unlikely. If not, he was to use the United States as a springboard for attacks against British and Spanish commerce and colonies: privateers would sail from American ports to prey on merchant vessels, while expeditions of American volunteers would invade Canada, Florida, and Louisiana. Money was yet another object. The French treasury was empty. The United States still owed France $5.6 million that it had borrowed to win independence. Genêt was instructed to coax the Americans to pay off that debt as quickly as possible.[2]

Genêt was treated as a hero in Charleston. Governor William Moultrie granted his request to outfit privateers to scour the seas of British shipping and bring them back to a prize court in Charleston. During his brief visit, Genêt commissioned four privateers before handing over the task to the French consul general. The French mission's subsequent cut of the loot would help underwrite other ambitions in the New World. Genêt announced his plan to raise two armies of American volunteers:

one to march overland and take East Florida, and the other to journey down the Mississippi and capture Louisiana. He fired off letters to prominent frontier leaders such as George Rogers Clark; designated them generals; gave them blank commissions to hand out to officers; promised ample funds to equip, feed, and transport their men; and dangled the vision of endless spoils after the conquest. Those blatant violations of American sovereignty would have been astonishing in any event, but especially since President Washington had not even officially received Genêt, let alone declared an official policy regarding the war.

Genêt released the *Embuscade* to sail north to Philadelphia and take any British merchant vessels that it encountered along the way, while he headed to the capital by land. He left Charleston by carriage on April 18 for a leisurely twenty-eight-day public relations campaign journey. On May 16, he rolled into Philadelphia through cheering crowds.

George Washington was at Mt. Vernon when, on April 13, he learned of France's war declaration against Britain. He rushed back to Philadelphia and, shortly after arriving on April 17, met with Hamilton. The next day he convened his cabinet and circulated a list of thirteen policy questions, which were most likely penned by Hamilton. Around the table sat Treasury Secretary Hamilton, Secretary of State Jefferson, War Secretary Knox, and Attorney General Randolph.[3]

One question underlay all others: what should America's position be toward the war in Europe? Hamilton's answer was that the nation's interests could be served only by declaring neutrality. Knox backed Hamilton. Although their hearts went out to France's revolutionaries, Republicans Jefferson and Randolph reluctantly went along as well.[4]

That policy foundation shaped answers to the rest of the questions. The next issue was whether the United States should even receive a minister from the French republic. The unanimous response was yes.

A stickler was whether in destroying the monarchy the French Revolution had eliminated any international legal duties accumulated by that regime wiped the legal slate clean with the previous regime of Louis XVI. Washington had partly resolved that question when, on March 12, 1793, he had Jefferson instruct Gouverneur Morris, America's minister in Paris, to convey the formal recognition of the National Assembly as France's legitimate government. But now Washington was clearly having second thoughts. Jefferson presented the winning argument that the United States had made treaties with a nation, not a government. Thus the 1778 alliance and commercial treaties were still valid.[5]

That posed the dilemma of how the United States could at once honor the 1778 alliance and America's very different interests in 1793. The alliance had been a lifesaver during the War for Independence; it was an albatross now. Washington and his cabinet finessed that question by agreeing that since France was the first to declare war, then it was the aggressor. The alliance required the parties to aid each other only if the other was attacked first.

But there was a much more serious potential catch. The commercial treaty that the United States had signed with France in 1778 permitted French privateers to use American ports for both supplies and prize courts and denied that privilege to France's enemies. This was Genêt's strongest diplomatic card, and he was playing it for all it was worth. How could the United States at once fulfill both its legal duty to France and its interest in maintaining a strict neutrality?

The consensus was that national interests must come first, with Hamilton and Knox agreeing emphatically, while Jefferson and Randolph were hesitant. Jefferson's argument that the United States should exchange neutrality for open markets with the belligerents did not carry the day. Hamilton objected that conducting multilateral negotiations with the warring states and forging the same deal among them would be nearly impossible. What would happen if one country agreed to open its markets and another did not? Should the United States remain neutral or side with the more generous country? Thus did unconditional neutrality prevail.

Then the question over just who could declare neutrality arose. Jefferson and Randolph argued that if the Constitution granted only Congress the power to declare war, it followed that only Congress could declare neutrality. Hamilton and Knox countered that since the Constitution does not explicitly grant Congress that power, then the executive can exercise it as one of his implied powers. Washington somewhat hesitantly sided with the latter view. They forged a compromise.

When the president issued on April 22, 1793, what became known as the "Neutrality Proclamation," in a nod to Jefferson and Randolph, it did not include the word *neutral*. The United States would "with sincerity and good faith adopt and pursue a conduct friendly and impartial toward the belligerent powers." To that end, Americans were forbidden to aid any side in that war; those who violated that policy risked punishment.

Federalists and Republicans split bitterly over the policy, with the former lauding and the latter condemning it. Under the pen name Helvidius, James Madison led the attack on the administration for its alleged sellout of an ally and fellow republican government. But the protests were in vain. Among the president's powers was to act as the nation's diplomat in chief. The Neutrality Proclamation was a legitimate expression of that power.[6]

The British, however, could be forgiven for dismissing Washington's proclamation as propaganda masking a policy tilted sharply toward France. Over the previous weeks, the *Embuscade* had captured several British vessels off the coast, brought them into American ports, and sold them and their cargoes. Within days after Washington declared neutrality, the *Embuscade* brought the *Grange* into Philadelphia. George Hammond, the British minister, issued a strong protest to Thomas Jefferson. The secretary of state informed French Minister Ternant on May 3 that the United States "being at peace with all the parties cannot see with indifference its territory or jurisdiction violated by either." It was not until May 18, however, that Jefferson told Ternant that the *Grange* would have to be released because it was taken in American waters. Ternant ordered the ship freed, but under protest. That would be Ternant's last act as French minister.[7]

That same day, Washington received Genêt. The new minister bore a very welcome gift to his host, word that his government had opened France's ports to American commerce without restriction on February 19. That very promising beginning did not last long. The Frenchman would swiftly wear out his welcome.

Few people who encountered Genêt went away without a strong opinion of the man. The spectrum of views ran from brilliant visionary to abrasive windbag. Genêt certainly did not mince his words about others, even his benefactors. Although the lacked diplomatic tact, he could be very perceptive. For instance, he aptly described Jefferson as "a man endowed with good qualities, but weak enough to sign what he does not believe and to defend officially threats which he condemns in his conversations and anonymous writings."[8]

With time, even once-fervent supporters began to weary of Genêt's incessant cajoling and intrigues. But for now, Republicans dined, wined, and toasted the French minister as a hero. All that adulation and the gravity of his mission went to his head. As for the Federalists, if they greeted him at all, they did so with icy reserve. That naturally turned Genêt exclusively to the adoring Republicans. Eventually he would alienate most of them as well.

The reason was more for hard political than for social reasons. Genêt resisted rather than adapted to a series of warnings from the administration. On June 5 Jefferson gave the Frenchman the bad news that the president had rejected his May 27 request that French privateers use American ports to war against Britain. On June 11 the secretary of state reluctantly shared with the minister another disappointment—the United States would not accelerate its debt payments to France. Jefferson penned a treatise that justified those policies and sent it to Genêt on June 17.[9]

Rather than gracefully accept those decisions, Genêt rebutted them on June 22. He appealed to Washington's government to "explain ourselves as republicans. Let us not lower ourselves to the level of ancient politics by diplomatic subtleties."

He recalled all the sacrifices that France had made for the United States, including human and financial during America's War for Independence, and the recent generosity of flinging open its markets to American trade.[10]

This appeal left Washington unmoved. After putting the finishing touches on policies toward France and other pressing matters, he departed on June 24 for Mount Vernon to tend his plantation.

The president's absence from the capital only emboldened Genêt. During a meeting between the Frenchman and the secretary of state on July 5, he shared with Jefferson the plan to gather a volunteer army in Kentucky that would descend the Ohio and Mississippi Rivers and take over Spain's Louisiana and West Florida territories. He then asked Jefferson to approve André Michaux, one of his agents and an acclaimed botanist, as a consul to Kentucky and once there promote the expedition.

The utter recklessness of Genêt's scheme stunned Jefferson. He replied that "his enticing officers & soldiers from Kentucky to go against Spain, was really putting a halter about their necks, for that they would assuredly be hung if they commenced hostilities against a nation at peace with the United States."[11]

Of that crucial meeting, Genêt recalled that Jefferson agreed with his scheme in principle but rejected it on practical grounds. The secretary of state explained that the United States had opened talks with Spain over the question of Mississippi River navigation and unloading goods at New Orleans. Thus the United States would not back taking by force what it might get by diplomacy.[12] He did agree to provide Michaux with a letter of introduction to Kentucky governor Isaac Shelby.

Genêt understandably interpreted Jefferson's words and letter to mean the United States might turn a blind eye to his scheme. So he hurried Michaux to Kentucky to enlist Shelby and other regional leaders as promoters of the proposed expedition. Had Genêt correctly read the often sphinxlike Jefferson? Jefferson clearly sympathized with the scheme even if he lacked the authority to approve it. Washington was upset when he learned of Michaux's mission. He had Jefferson send a request to Shelby that he prevent any recruiting for the expedition. Orders were sent to Arthur St. Clair, the governor of the Northwest Territory, and Maj. Gen. Anthony Wayne to intercept and turn back any expedition that was headed toward the Spanish empire.[13]

In the end, nothing of substance ever came of Michaux's mission. George Rogers Clark, the Revolutionary War hero whom the French hoped would conquer Louisiana and the Floridas for them, was now a pathetic alcoholic and incapable of mustering the charisma, energy, and vision he had displayed fifteen years before during the Revolution. Nonetheless, the rumors of the expedition provoked fear among the Spanish.

What Genêt did next ruined whatever vague support he had from Jefferson. Sitting in Philadelphia's harbor was the British merchant ship *Little Sarah*, which the *Embuscade* had recently taken. The French had renamed their prize the *Petite Democrate* and were converting it into a warship.

Fearing that to allow the French privateer to put to sea would open Pennsylvania to British retaliation, Governor Thomas Mifflin sent his secretary of state, Alexander Dallas, to Genêt on July 7 with a request that he keep that vessel in port. This enraged Genêt, who threatened to hasten its sailing date. The governor appealed to the secretary of state, who promptly summoned the French minister. Genêt rejected Jefferson's plea that he desist until the president returned to the capital and judged the matter.

In doing so, Genêt bit the most vital political hand that had been feeding him. Now even Jefferson turned against him, although his Francophilia and Anglophobia remained equally fervent. He wrote Madison, "Never . . . was so calamitous an appointment made." He lamented that Genêt was "hotheaded, all imagination, no judgment, passionate, disrespectful, & even indecent toward the President in his written as well as verbal communications."[14]

Genêt acted on his threat. The word that the *Petite Democrate* was preparing to sail provoked a crisis that was exacerbated by the president's absence. Hamilton, Jefferson, Knox, and Mifflin met to debate what to do. Hamilton and Knox took a tough line by calling for the privateer to be stopped by force. Jefferson and Mifflin preferred a diplomatic solution. As they debated, the *Petite Democrate* unfurled sails, slipped down the Delaware River, and cruised out to the open sea.

As if the use or abuse, depending on one's view, of American ports by French privateers was not troubling enough, the shifting policy of the French government, now known as the Convention, toward neutral shipping raised serious problems. American merchants rejoiced when they learned that on February 19, 1793, Paris had opened French colonies to American trade. They were later stunned to hear that on May 9, 1793, the Convention had decreed that French warships and privateers could seize any neutral ships bound for Britain. Gouverneur Morris and other prominent members of the American community in Paris protested that policy as a blatant violation of the 1778 commercial treaty. The French government agreed to exempt American vessels on May 23, then reversed course on July 27 by asserting that all neutral ships carrying any war contraband, including food, were subject to seizure. The French justified their July 27 policy as a reaction to Whitehall's Order in Council of June 8, 1793, which declared neutral trade with France fair game for Britain's warships and privateers. Over the next twenty-two years, the British would sweep more than twice as many American merchant vessels from the sea as the French, provoking twice as many enraged protests from the victims for compensation and an end to the depredations.[15]

Washington would not learn the details of the policies of France or Britain toward neutral shipping until later. But he had plenty to be angry about when he returned to Philadelphia on July 11 and studied the reports on Genêt's machinations by Hamilton, Knox, and Jefferson.[16] "Is the Minister of the French Republic to set the acts of this Government at defiance with impunity?" he roared. "What would the world think of such conduct, and of the Government of the United States in submitting to it?"[17]

The president convened a cabinet meeting the next morning. Hamilton suggested asking the French government to recall Genêt. A majority opted to shelve that proposal for now. Instead they agreed that the secretary of state should write Genêt a stern letter condemning him for letting the *Petite Democrate* sail away.[18]

The question of the Neutrality Proclamation's legality and substance continued to nag the president and his men. They decided to ask the Supreme Court to render its opinion on those issues. Although an official response would not be issued until August 8, shortly after receiving the petition on July 18, Chief Justice John Jay privately explained his belief that the Supreme Court lacked explicit constitutional authority to make a decision on the matter.[19]

Jay's hesitancy forced the president and his cabinet to roll up their sleeves and draft their own detailed document on neutrality. Hamilton was the chief author of the "Rules Governing Belligerents," which was issued on August 4. All warring countries were barred from outfitting warships in American ports or seizing prizes in American waters. The Treasury Department's revenue officials rather than the state governments would enforce the policy.[20]

Meanwhile, another controversy erupted. Two Americans had enlisted on the French privateer *Citizen Genêt*. Philadelphia authorities arrested them for violating the president's Neutrality Proclamation after they stepped ashore in the city. Genêt immediately took up their defense. He argued that first of all, a proclamation was a statement of principles and not legally binding. He then pointed out that there was no law on the federal or state books that prevented foreigners from recruiting Americans nor Americans from enlisting in a foreign army or navy. Genêt was absolutely right on both counts. After two days of deliberation, a jury dismissed the case against the sailors. With that legal wind behind him, Genêt redoubled his efforts to recruit Americans through public meetings and advertisements.

The series of French intrigues had strained the cabinet's patience to the snapping point. On July 23 Washington reached for Hamilton's proposal that had been shelved ten days earlier. The cabinet swiftly reached a consensus that Genêt had to go. They would assemble and translate all the documents revealing Genêt's machinations since he first set foot in the United States. Jefferson would write a cover letter and send the package to Gouverneur Morris, who would present it to the Foreign Ministry in Paris and ask for Genêt's recall. That task was not done until August 16, however.[21]

The only trouble with a formal recall was that it would be months before they learned whether Paris would honor it. In the meantime, Genêt could commit plenty of mischief. He had already exacerbated bitter debates among Americans and had skirted the edges of the law. His revolutionary fervor inspired many Americans to want to somehow revive their own revolutionary past. Republicans excitedly compared the French Jacobins to America's Sons of Liberty a generation earlier.

This revolutionary fervor inspired the founding of the Democratic Society, modeled on France's radical Jacobin Party, in Philadelphia in May 1793. Edmond Genêt not only was present at the creation but also had suggested its name. The Democratic Society sent invitations to prominent Republicans across the country to form branches. About ten other democratic societies were founded later that year and twice as many more the next year. While most members claimed to be nonpartisan, the clubs were clearly linked by ideology, people, and money to the Republican Party. They would help mobilize protests against the whiskey tax and Jay Treaty and masses of voters for elections.[22]

The Federalists tried and failed to create their own grassroots organizations. The Constitutional Association of Elizabethtown, New Jersey, and the Society of Constitutional and Governmental Support of Norfolk, Virginia, were too cerebral and elitist to attract a mass following in their respective towns, let alone to sow branches across the nation. So, to mobilize the masses, the Federalists had to rely all the more on their newspapers, such as John Fenno's *Gazette of the United States* in Philadelphia, Noah Webster's *American Minerva* of New York, and Benjamin Russell's *Columbian Centinel* of Boston.

These newspapers exacerbated a very public debate that had all along paralleled and often intersected with the secret cabinet policy discussions.[23] The first shots in the battle had appeared the first two weeks of June in Republican Philip Freneau's *National Gazette*. In four essays "Veritas" (whose identity is still unknown) had championed the French Revolution and Genêt's mission and called on Americans to give all possible aid short of war to their fellow republicans.

This provoked Hamilton to launch a counterattack as "Publicus" through seven essays from June 29 through July 27 in the *Gazette of the United States*. Hamilton essentially articulated what would become the 1794 Neutrality Act. His key argument was that national interests trumped all other concerns: "Self-preservation is the first duty of a nation. Good faith does not require that the United States should put in jeopardy their essential interests . . . to secure to France, what?"[24]

Hamilton's essays were so intellectually powerful that Jefferson feared they were inflicting knockout blows on Veritas, so he called Madison into the ring. Writing five essays as "Helvidius," Madison emphasized anti-Federalist ideals of limited, decentralized government and charged the administration with assuming unconstitutional powers. The Neutrality Proclamation did not negate America's legal duties to France under the 1778 alliance and commercial treaties, and thus those must be honored.[25]

Jefferson opened another front in the policy war when he passed word to the democratic societies to escalate their attacks on Federalists. Here the Federalists, not having any equivalent grassroots organizations, were completely outgunned. So Hamilton sought to trump the Republican offensives across the board by releasing all information on Genêt's machinations. If the public knew the sordid truth, their outcry might silence or at least drown out the Republicans. Washington was inclined to agree.

This terrified Jefferson. He sent word to Madison that "we have decided unanimously to require the recall of Genêt. He will sink the republican interest if they do not abandon him." But he had to prevent the whole story about Genêt from getting out. At this point he had only one card to play, but it was powerful. He sent word to the president that he would retire in September. Washington met with Jefferson on August 6 and implored him to stay. A deal was cut whereby Jefferson would remain in office until January 1, 1794, and would ask sympathetic editors and the democratic societies to mute their cheering of Genêt if Washington repressed the bombshell information about the minister.[26]

Jefferson was faithful to only part of the deal. Although he stayed in office until the new year, he actually called on Madison to spread the word to the Democratic Societies to broaden and intensify their attacks on the Federalists. Their followers were to "abandon Genêt entirely," while expressing "strong friendship & adherence to his nation & confidence he has acted against their sense. In this way we shall keep the people on our side by keeping ourselves in the right."[27]

Yellow fever brought a fleeting abatement to the political war in Philadelphia, if nowhere else. The outbreak in September and October killed more than four thousand people and caused John Fenno to shut down his press for months and Philip Freneau to do so permanently. This dried up national political stories for Republican and Federalists newspapers alike across the country, since they often copied verbatim stories that appeared in the two *Gazettes*.

The dearth of news from Philadelphia may have caused readers to pay closer attention to events further afield. A story out of Boston rankled the president. Antoine Duplaine, the French consul general, was not just blatantly violating the neutrality policy by helping arm and supply privateers. At one point, he had actually mustered men from a French warship in harbor to liberate a vessel that had been impounded by Boston authorities. The federal district attorney had Duplaine arrested and tried three times, only to be enraged as sympathetic juries acquitted him.

This provoked Washington to finally take off his diplomatic gloves. He declared Duplaine persona non grata and had Jefferson send to the other consuls general a circular letter clearly explaining the dos and don'ts of their position and pointing to Duplaine's behavior as an example of what not to do.[28]

Genêt shrilly protested, an act that only attracted the president's stern gaze. Washington could only inwardly rejoice that the intriguer's time was most likely short. He and his men had kept secret their request to recall Genêt. They worried that if he believed he had nothing to lose, he might risk all. He would certainly send his own version of events to Paris and thus possibly prevent his recall. But now that the ship carrying Jefferson's letter and evidence had sailed, Washington changed his mind. Perhaps with a hint of glee, he had Jefferson inform Genêt on September 15 that an official request had been sent to Paris for his recall. The Frenchman fired a heated protest back to Jefferson that condemned the president for the act. Washington could keep his patience only until December. At that time he would lay the Genêt documents before Congress when it reconvened, and the world would learn of all the indignities that the president and the nation had suffered since Genêt had first set foot in America.[29]

Morris received the package and hurried it to the Foreign Ministry on October 8. The embarrassed response was that the French government would promptly recall Genêt. Washington would have the pleasure of relaying that good news to Congress on January 20, 1794.[30]

Genêt's machinations had spotlighted all the problems of guarding the nation's neutrality. It had been easy enough to issue a declaration. The devil inevitably was in managing the details and dealing with wild cards like Genêt and Duplaine. Some questions were easier to answer than others. For instance, Washington and his cabinet had soon concluded that foreigners could not set up admiralty courts in American ports to rule on prizes. They had also agreed that if the United States was neutral, it could not be used as a platform for land or sea attacks by one belligerent against the other.

But one question eluded a swift answer. If American waters were off-limits to engagements between the belligerents, then just how far out to sea did the nation's sovereignty extend? It took Washington and his men seven months to reach a consensus. In November 1793 the administration announced that henceforth the United States would assert a one-league or three-mile territorial sea from the nation's shores. That distance was about the farthest the largest cannons of that era could fire a ball and thus control the sea beyond one's shores.

A continual Federalist assertion was that the nation's diplomatic hand was only as strong as its military power. In his December 3, 1793, address to Congress, the president warned,

> I cannot recommend to your notice measures for the fulfillment of our duties to the rest of the world without again pressing upon you the necessity of placing ourselves in a condition of complete defense, and of extracting from them the fulfillment of their duties toward us. If we desire to avoid insult, we must be able to repel it; if we desire to secure peace, one of the most powerful instruments of our rising prosperity, it must be known, that we are at all times ready for war.[31]

He asked Congress to appropriate money to fill the nation's arsenals with arms and munitions, reorganize the militia, launch a program to build six frigates, and establish a military academy.

Nearly a year after Washington first declared neutrality, he issued a second declaration on March 24, 1794. This time he specifically stated that foreigners were forbidden from recruiting Americans to war against countries that were friendly to the United States. He warned that any men who had enlisted in Genêt's schemes to attack Louisiana and the Floridas would be arrested and prosecuted. That policy became the foundation for the Neutrality Act passed by Congress on June 5, 1794.[32]

Jean Antoine Joseph Fauchet arrived on February 21, 1794, with orders to apprehend Genêt and replace him as minister. Genêt prudently refused to surrender himself into Fauchet's custody. Fauchet asked Washington to issue an order for Genêt's arrest. The president politely refused to do so. He was well aware that a guillotine awaited Genêt back in Paris.

The worst of France's revolution had come. The Jacobins had exploited the fear of foreign invasion to amass dictatorial powers and crush anyone who disagreed with them. They ruled through a twelve-man Committee of Public Safety chaired by Maximilien Robespierre. On September 5, 1793, Robespierre and the others unleashed what they called "the terror" against their political opponents. Over the next eleven months, until the Jacobins were overthrown on July 28, 1794, thousands of people were rounded up and summarily executed.

Thanks to George Washington's clemency, Genêt's fate was a happy one. He fell in love with Cornelia Clinton, the daughter of New York Republican governor George Clinton; married her later that year; and retired from public life to a prosperous farm overlooking the Hudson River at East Greenbush, New York. He became an American citizen in 1804 and died in 1834.

There had been irony in Gouverneur Morris's assignment to ask for Genêt's recall. Fauchet's next order of business after asking for Genêt's arrest was to ask for Morris's recall. Washington reluctantly agreed to what was in effect a quid pro quo.[33]

Morris had been as much a thorn in the Jacobins' side as Genêt had been to the Federalists. It was well known that he had conspired with the royalists and moderates against the radicals. Only his diplomatic immunity had prevented the Jacobins from expelling him or worse. Morris was the first to admit that they "hate me cordially, tho it would puzzle them to say why."[34] Actually they would have given him an earful, had he bothered to ask. Morris was well aware that Fauchet was going to demand his recall. In April 1793 he sought refuge at his mansion at Sainport, on the bank of the Seine twenty miles downriver from Paris. Although he continued his intrigues there, the Jacobins left him alone. He received word that he was being recalled, but his replacement, James Monroe, would not arrive until August 1794.[35]

The resolution of the Genêt problem and neutrality question gave little relief to Washington and his advisers. A potentially even more dangerous problem was demanding ever more of their time and efforts.

11

British Aggression
and Trade War

The Genêt imbroglio obscured for a while the impact of a shift in British policy. Whitehall's Order in Council of June 8, 1793, authorized British warships and privateers to seize all neutral ships carrying war contraband, including food, bound for French ports. This policy would devastate American merchants because a large portion of their exports were grain, dried fish, salted beef, rum, and other provisions. Then, atop that, on November 6, 1793, another Order in Council targeted any neutral ship carrying anything to any French colony. The British delayed announcing the policy for a month to give its warships and privateers enough time to pounce on unsuspecting American and other foreign ships. Finally, the British did not only confiscate goods. In British ports press gangs were rounding up American sailors and forcing them to serve His Majesty's navy. Eventually Whitehall would extend that practice to the high seas.

The practical justifications for such policies were clear enough. By taking goods bound to France, Britain at once strengthened itself and weakened its enemy. Foreign Secretary William Wyndham, Lord Grenville, explained to George Hammond, the minister to the United States, that not doing so would allow "the French those means of Subsistence, and of carrying on the war, which, from the nature of their present situation, and of the Force employed against them, they must otherwise be unable to procure."[1] Besides, the government was in ever more desperate need of money. The admiralty courts would split the value of a legal prize equally between the government and privateer and pay the full cost of the ship illegally seized; formerly, privateers had enjoyed the full prize but also bore the full cost of an illegal seizure. Now the government enjoyed some badly needed revenues. In addition, impressment helped fill the vessels of an ever-expanding Royal Navy.

Whitehall also made a legal case for those policies. Retaliation in kind was an accepted principle and practice of international law. The Orders in Council were merely necessary responses to two French policies that had been announced earlier that year. On February 19, 1793, the Convention had declared that France's colonial ports would be opened to neutral foreign traders. This violated Britain's Rule of 1756, which stated that ports closed to foreign traders in peace should remain closed in war. This policy prevented a blockaded country from evading the blockade. The British claimed that their rule had become an accepted international custom and thus an unwritten international law, but all other seafaring nations disputed this argument. Then, on May 9, 1793, the Convention declared that its privateers and warships could seize any neutral ships bound for enemy ports and carrying contraband of war, including food. So Britain's policy simply mirrored French policy, at least for a while. But they carried on that policy even after the French lifted the embargo on neutral trade with Britain on April 6, 1794.

The impact of Whitehall's Orders in Council would far exceed France's seesaw policies toward neutral trade. Over the next twenty-two years, British warships and privateers, would capture more than twice as many American vessels as French warships and privateers, and thus provoke far more American hatred and demands for compensation and vengeance. Crews were tossed into prison while an admiralty court determined the fate of a vessel's cargo. If a cargo was condemned, the sailors had to find their own way home. Many never made it; they either died of tropical diseases or were herded onto British warships. There was a political uproar when word of these depredations reached the United States. But without a powerful navy, the United States could protest only in vain.[2]

As early as 1792, Jefferson had Thomas Pinckney, America's minister in London, issue the first official protest against British impressment.[3] Whitehall retorted that cases of mistaken identity could be alleviated if American seamen carried papers certifying their nationality. Jefferson rejected this advice on practical and legal grounds, although injured pride may have also been an important factor. Even if documents that proved a sailor's citizenship existed, the time and expense for him to get them would be an unjustified intrusion. But for many, such proof no longer or ever existed, or could not be found.

Given their aversion to a strong military, the Republicans had only one card to play against Britain. Jefferson's last act as secretary of state was to provide Madison and the Republicans with ammunition to launch their campaign to force reciprocity from Britain by denying them trade with the United States. On December

16, 1793, he released the "Report on the Privileges and Restrictions on the Commerce of the United States." Although the report offered a wide-ranging overview of the subject, it condemned British mercantilist policies for deliberately trying to contain American commercial power by depriving the United States of markets. Since the Americans had won independence, their exports had not grown as fast as their imports, and the fledgling country remained dependent on Britain for about 75 percent of its trade. The British further skewed that trade in their favor by letting only raw materials into their home markets and completely excluding Americans from the West Indies.[4]

With Jefferson retired at Monticello, James Madison was now the Republican leader. He opened his offensive on January 3, 1794, by presenting to the House of Representatives seven resolutions that called for "reciprocity" between the United States and all other nations. To pressure foreigners into reciprocating, he advocated raising duties for those who discriminated against the United States and cutting duties for those states that complied with the policy. The extra revenues would compensate American shippers that had suffered losses at British hands.[5]

With a Republican majority behind him, Madison's resolutions had enormous political power as well as emotional appeal. Unfortunately, as historians Stanley Elkins and Eric McKitrick point out, "Madison's case did not hold up at all: his figures were either wrong or obsolete, his reasoning was dotted with fallacies, and his knowledge of the state of trade and shipping was very shaky. . . . Madison's was not an economic case but a moral one."[6]

At the Treasury Department, Hamilton had extensive and accurate trade statistics at his fingertips. These revealed that American trade had actually been increasing since 1787 and had jumped after war broke out in Europe in 1792 as ever-more merchant houses in all the warring states switched to America's neutral ships to carry their goods. In 1792 the United States exported $8,260,463 of goods to Britain and imported $15,285,426 for a deficit of $7,024,963. With France, America's exports were $5,243,543 and imports were $2,069,348, for a $3,174,195 surplus. America's $23,545,889 trade with Britain was three times larger than its $7,312,891 trade with France. Although America was still dependent on British markets, it was steadily diversifying its exports across the Atlantic, Caribbean, Mediterranean, and even Pacific basins. The percentage of American ships carrying American trade rose from 58.6 percent in 1790 to an astonishing 93.1 percent in 1796. Profits for American traders had never been higher. This in turn inspired a building boom for ships, whose demand for goods and services rippled through the eastern seaboard economies and beyond. Rather deceptively, Jefferson's December 16 report neglected these recent figures.[7]

Hamilton's point men in Congress for countering Madison were William Loughton Smith of South Carolina and Fisher Ames of Massachusetts. Both used the treasury report to eviscerate Madison's arguments. The seemingly soft spot in the Federalist position was the severe trade deficit with Britain. The Federalists explained that the trade deficit with Britain was understandable given that the British produced goods that Americans did not yet make for themselves. This unhappy situation could one day be reversed if Congress adopted the industrial revolution advocated by Hamilton in his "Report on Manufacturing." Britain also enjoyed a financial advantage over the United States; British firms had deep pockets and thus could offer credit to buyers, something few American firms could do. But Hamilton's financial revolution would eventually allow American firms to match and even surpass their British rivals. The Federalists rejected Madison's proposed duties because they only burdened American buyers and did not hurt British producers. Ames summed up the Federalist argument by asking, "We are being invited to engage in a contest of self-denial. For what?"[8]

Although the House voted 61 to 47 to table Madison's proposal, a cry soon arose to take even firmer measures. Reports arrived that British warships were capturing American merchant vessels in the Caribbean. Then, on March 7, 1794, word reached Philadelphia of Britain's latest Order in Council. Henceforth the British would confiscate any ships trading with France regardless of the cargo. Whitehall had officially adopted the policy on November 6, 1793, but did not publicize it until December to let the British fleet cast their net before the vessels could escape to safe ports. By early spring the British had scoured the seas of over 250 ships.[9]

Hamilton got tough with the British. The following day, he advised Washington to ask Congress to boost America's army to twenty thousand troops, fortify the principal ports, build a half dozen frigates, and empower the president to sever trade with Britain. This should have forever laid to rest, among reasonable minds, the smear that Hamilton was an Anglophile who promoted British interests. Having already called for a similar measure to no effect, Washington did not want to risk his prestige again. So Hamilton convinced Representative Theodore Sedgwick of Massachusetts to spearhead the bill through the House.[10]

This put Madison and the Republicans in a political bind. They wanted to stand up to the British as long as it did not cost any money, bolster the military, or threaten war. Madison complained to Jefferson that the Federalists "are endeavoring to take the lead in defensive preparations, and to acquire merit with the people by anticipating their wishes." He claimed that the proposal was simply an old Federalist "trick of turning every contingency into a resource for accumulating force in the Government." So Madison spurned the Federalist measure and continued to insist that his own proposal was the answer. The result was deadlock, as neither proposal could garner enough votes for passage.[11]

Amid that debate more bad news arrived on March 20. Canadian governor Guy Carleton, Lord Dorchester, and Lieutenant Governor John Simcoe were riling up the Indians against the Americans in the Northwest Territory. On February 10 Dorchester made an inflammatory speech at Quebec before an Indian council in which he condemned the United States, predicted that a war would break out that year, and urged the Indians to assure that the Americans "lose all their improvements and houses on our side of [the frontier]; those People must be all gone, who do not obtain leave to become the king's subjects; what belongs to the Indians will of course be confirmed and secured to them."[12]

Dorchester was playing a dangerous diplomatic game. His words were intended solely for the Indians' ears. He sought to divert Indian rage against the United States and keep American settlers away from Canada's borders for as long as possible. Yet he was also bound to avoid war between Britain and America at all costs.

The governor's oration did not just impassion the Indians. Wielding a copy of Dorchester's speech like a red flag, Madison rallied enough votes in the House on March 25 to pass a one-month embargo on American shipping. Most of the Senate agreed the following day. Washington signed the bill into law. This encouraged Republicans to take another retaliatory step. A bill was drawn up to sequester all money that Americans owed Britain and use it to compensate American merchants who had lost vessels and cargoes to British depredations.

Tensions eased somewhat on March 28 with word that Whitehall had issued a new Order in Council on January 8, 1794. Rather than seize all ships sailing to France's West Indian colonies, the British would capture only those en route between the islands and France. That change in policy was brought about by pressure on Prime Minister William Pitt from British merchants who feared losing their markets in the United States should an embargo or war break out. A report on that new policy, along with a conciliatory message from Grenville, arrived from Thomas Pinckney on April 4.

Yet the damage to American shipping had already been done. The Republicans were not willing to threaten war with Britain, but they would be happy to cut off all trade indefinitely. Abraham Clark of New Jersey proposed on April 7 a resolution that would suspend all trade with Britain until it compensated the owners of the ships that had been seized, and evacuated the posts in the Northwest Territory. On April 15 the House passed by 54 to 44 a bill that would sever trade with Britain for two months.

Through these weeks of mounting rage in Congress, Washington despaired over what to do. He feared that the ever-tougher retaliatory measures might lead to war. Yet he recognized that the United States had no choice but to defend itself from British attacks on American shipping and honor. As usual, Hamilton's advice decided the issue. He presented an airtight analysis and suggested that the president appoint John Jay as a special envoy empowered to resolve all outstanding conflicts with Britain. After convincing a reluctant Jay to accept the mission, Washington sent his name to the Senate for confirmation. The Senate approved by a vote of 18 to 8 on April 19, 1794.[13]

Madison in turn tabled the sequestration bill and amended the embargo bill so that the cutoff date was November 1, 1794. Although he and most of his fellow Republicans opposed a bill to build six state-of-the-art frigates, four of forty-four guns and two of thirty-six guns, a slender majority in each house voted in favor; Washington signed that bill into law on March 27, 1794. Congress also passed Sedgwick's bill to raise the army's authorized strength from 3,861 to 25,000, backed by 80,000 militia under federal control. That army strength would hold for the next two years and then expire unless Congress saw fit to extend it. Although Congress eventually appropriated enough funds to lay the keels for three of the frigates, they never budgeted for the expanded army.

All this gave Jay a measure of bargaining power. Eventually Congress and the nation would find out just what John Jay did with the powers and instructions he was granted. Most would not be pleased.

12

The Whiskey Rebellion

T he fate of America's trans-Appalachian territory was a perennial concern during the early republic. The economic and political links between the eastern seaboard and western settlements were fragile and fraying. The westerners felt that easterners were indifferent to them and had all but abandoned them first during the War for Independence and now during the Northwest Indian War. Kentuckian John Breckinridge captured their views: "Nature has done everything for us; Government everything against us."[1]

Those widespread beliefs were, of course, nonsense. The government had sent what troops and supplies that it could spare during both wars. But westerners nurtured a hatred of government and a myth of independence that defied reason and facts. These sentiments were so powerful that many spoke openly of breaking away from the United States and forming their own country or joining the British or Spanish empires, and some, like James Wilkinson, secretly conspired with foreign powers.

Westerners were hypersensitive to what they believed were insults or exploitation from easterners. In their eyes, Alexander Hamilton committed just such an assault when, in 1791, he convinced Congress to impose an excise tax on whiskey, a key product of the western economy.[2] Because farmers beyond the Appalachian Mountains could not easily transport their corn surpluses to eastern markets, many distilled their surplus into whiskey and sold it locally. The excise tax was passed on to consumers who bellowed at the rise in prices. The first sporadic protests and violence arose in the upper Ohio River Valley, where the distilleries were the most densely located, with Pittsburgh the epicenter, in the summer of 1791. But there was not yet an organized movement, only a general burning resentment against eastern politicians. In May 1792 Congress amended the bill so that the tax was lowered, but that did little to dampen the anger. For the next two years western farmers held occasional rallies and petitions and, more rarely, tarred and feathered excise officers.

What became known as the Whiskey Rebellion did not erupt until the summer of 1794, when the federal government made a concerted attempt to enforce the law. Once again resentment only transformed into violence in the upper Ohio River Valley. U.S. Marshal David Lenox and Excise Inspector John Neville had been issuing writs against those farmers who had not registered their stills. A mob of nearly five hundred men attacked Neville's home on July 16, 1794. With Neville were a few friends and a dozen soldiers from nearby from Fort Pitt. They opened fired on the mob, killing two and wounding six. Neville somehow escaped while the others surrendered. The rebels held Lenox hostage and looted and burned the house.

When word of the insurrection reached Philadelphia on July 25, a debate erupted within the administration, Congress, and beyond over what to do. At stake was not merely a legal matter but a profound question of just what were the federal government's powers and duties. Federalists and Republicans squared off and asserted their respective positions.

The battle lines within Washington's cabinet were predictable. The Federalists Hamilton and Knox favored a tough assertion of federal power to crush the rebellion, while the Republican Randolph called for leaving the matter in Pennsylvania's hands. As usual, Hamilton's argument prevailed. Appeasement, the treasury secretary argued, would merely encourage other disaffected groups to defy the government. He and Knox calculated that about 12,400 militia from Pennsylvania, New Jersey, Maryland, and Virginia could smother the rebellion. Washington agreed but was legally constrained from acting immediately.[3]

The Constitution designates a president the nation's commander in chief and empowers him to call "forth the Militia to execute the Laws of the Union, suppress rebellions, and repel invasions." The document is silent on how long and where the militia must serve. The 1792 Militia Act was an attempt both to clarify and contain the government's power to muster the militia. Under that bill, a federal judge must rule that law and order has broken down before a president or governor can act. Washington thus had to await a ruling by Justice James Wilson. After reviewing all the available reports, Wilson declared on August 4 that law and order had indeed broken down.[4]

The next step was for the president to coordinate any actions with Pennsylvania governor Thomas Mifflin. Ideally the governor would call out the troops and crush the rebellion himself. But as a Republican, Mifflin was a fervent states' righter and populist, and thus opposed any action. As an excuse, he told Washington that he was reluctant to muster the militia for fear they would not show up. Left unsaid was that he wanted the Washington administration and Federalist Party to take the blame for marching against fellow Americans.[5]

Washington wisely chose to wield both the carrot and stick in putting down the rebellion. He gave the rebels until September 1 to lay down their arms and pay the tax; otherwise, the militia would march against them. The deadline passed. Washington then waited two weeks before issuing a proclamation that declared martial law for the Pittsburgh region. He sent the militia westward from Philadelphia on September 25; the president set off five days later to catch up with them at Carlisle, the expedition's staging area. Washington turned over the command to Maj. Gen. Henry Lee and returned to the capital. The rebels had mostly dispersed long before Lee's militia army arrived. A dozen men were arrested and brought back to Philadelphia for trial. Only two were found guilty of treason, and they eventually received presidential pardons.

Although neither the rebellion nor the crackdown amounted to much, the results were important. By acting decisively with concerted administrative, judicial, diplomatic, and military means, George Washington further clarified the hazy executive powers latent in the Constitution. But in doing so he had to endure a barrage of Republican attacks on his policy and character.

These attacks deeply embittered Washington. He associated the Whiskey rebels, the Democratic Societies, Genêt, and the Jacobins as all interconnected and dangerous to American security and liberty. He publicly condemned the Democratic Societies for having "enflamed the insurrection, for some of the leaders of those societies had likewise been the leaders of the riots." He feared that if the societies were not subdued they would "shake the government to its foundation," and thus America would "bid adieu to all government in this Country, except mob and club government."[6] While Washington did not deny the Democratic Societies the right of assembly, he feared they were abusing that right by conspiring against the government. The Federalists shared that fear; the Republicans denied any conspiracy.

13

Winning the West

Whitehall officially favored peace on the American frontier. Nothing, of course, could have been more contrary to British interests. With each peace treaty, the Indians ceded territory to the land-hungry Americans. Each peace was no more than a truce, as Americans not only poured into the newly won territory but also spilled over into adjacent Indian lands. That infiltration of hunters, trappers, traders, and squatters provoked worsening tension with the tribes that would sooner or later explode into war, with an inevitable result. The Indians would lose the war, surrender more land, and retreat further west. So Britain's not so secret policy was to supply the arms, munitions, and encouragement for warriors to ravage the American frontier as far from Canadian territory as possible. Meanwhile, British merchants could continue to reap riches from the fur trade, unmolested by their American rivals, in Indian lands on American territory.[1]

Alexander McKee was Britain's deputy Indian superintendent at Detroit. His duty was to maintain the loyalty of the northwest tribal coalition at all costs. Those costs were exorbitant. It took huge piles of trade goods to get the Indians' attention, let alone their allegiance. Whitehall dutifully sent annually to Canada the shiploads of goods vital for Indian diplomacy.

Given all that, the British had more than a slight conflict of interest when American secretary of war Henry Knox asked British minister George Hammond for Britain's help in ending the war with the northwest Indians. President Washington had appointed three peace commissioners—Benjamin Lincoln,

Beverley Randolph, and Timothy Pickering. He hoped that the envoys could travel via the Great Lakes and secure safe passage with letters of introduction from Hammond and John Simcoe, Upper Canada's governor. Knox assured Hammond that these men were "selected because they do not entertain unfavorable dispositions toward Great Britain."[2] Hammond agreed and wrote a letter. This would be the only easy part of the Americans' latest attempts at diplomacy.

The Washington administration had no choice in using the British as intermediaries. The president had previously enlisted the Iroquois, or Six Nations, as go-betweens, but their most prominent leader, Joseph Brant, had failed to forge an agreement between the Americans and the northwest tribes; Brant blamed McKee for encouraging the Indians not to make peace.[3] An attempt at direct talks had ended in tragedy. The Indians had murdered two previous, separate pairs of officers who had journeyed to their villages under truce flags. Even if Washington's latest envoys were under British protection, their odds of success were reckoned at nearly nil—the Indian hatred and suspicions of Americans were too great. Pickering explained to Washington, "Indians have been so deceived by White people, that White Man is, among many of them, another name for liar."[4]

With their predecessors' fate in mind, the three commissioners embarked with enormous trepidation on the long hard trip to Fort Niagara, where the Niagara River flows into Lake Ontario. However arduous their physical journey over the next four months, it would pale beside their diplomatic trials. The envoys were all bright, worldly men. But they would be captive to the wiles of a succession of tough British frontier agents who did all they could to discourage, bewilder, misinform, and frighten them.

Simcoe was their first formidable host. Lincoln and Pickering reached Fort Niagara on May 23, 1793, and Randolph a few days later. They asked Simcoe to provide them a military escort to the Northwest Territory. Simcoe promised to do so when he could spare the troops. The Americans swallowed hard at that obvious ploy. Surely a dozen redcoats and an officer could be culled from the scores manning the post. But it would not do to belabor the point. After all, they were in Simcoe's power. If they offended him, he could simply send them packing back home. Ironically, their only diplomatic card was to be as humble and patient as possible; this tactic might eventually wear down Simcoe to finally give in and send them farther west.

Simcoe kept them at Fort Niagara for six weeks before he finally permitted them to proceed. It was not until July 11 that the envoys set forth with their escort, first by horseback from Fort Niagara along the spectacular Niagara River gorge and past the falls to Lake Erie. From there it was ten days of hard rowing to the

Detroit River. But Fort Detroit's commander, Col. Arent Schuyler de Peyster, forbade them to ascend to Detroit itself. Instead they had to cool their heels at the nearby home of Indian agent Matthew Elliott.

Detroit was the trade and diplomatic center for the vast upper Great Lakes region, and the commissioners tried to hide their disappointment when that venue was denied them. Besides Detroit, there were two other prominent council sites in the region. Clearings near the Sandusky River mouth and Auglaize at the Maumee River rapids were traditional gathering grounds where the tribes discussed vital issues. The envoys sent messages to the tribes asking them to meet at either council ground. They waited two weeks before replies began to arrive.

A northwest Indian delegation strode into Elliott's home on July 30. The meeting was brief. The Indians insisted on the Ohio and Allegheny River boundary. The Americans pointed out that under a succession of treaties culminating with the most recent at Fort Harmar in 1789, the tribes had actually ceded land from the Cuyahoga River to its headwaters, then west to the Miami River headwaters, and then southeast until it hit the Ohio River at the Kentucky River mouth on the south bank. The Indian envoys angrily declared that their tribal councils had refused to ratify those treaties. When neither side would yield to the other, the Indians warned the envoys that they stayed in Indian land at their peril, and departed. The Americans headed back on the long trek to Philadelphia. With the diplomatic option dead, the Washington administration could only hope for a military solution.

To prepare and lead the Legion, Maj. Gen. Anthony Wayne combined his own military experience with wisdom from Caesar's commentaries. He drilled his troops for several hours each day, both for parade ground reviews and wilderness battle tactics. On the march and at camp, the companies were deployed in a square with the supplies and draft animals sheltered within; a makeshift wall of logs surrounded every camp.

The war was hardly on hold as Wayne prepared the Legion. Indian raids struck vulnerable settlements and left mutilated bodies and smoldering ruins behind. Political pressure, especially from Kentucky, which was the hardest hit, to hurry up and march built on Wayne. To those demands, Wayne replied with diminishing patience that the Legion would march only when it was ready.

Wayne began his slow, methodical advance northward from the camp near Fort Washington on October 7, 1793. His 2,600 troops averaged a half-dozen or so miles a day and built a fort every score of miles. Eighty miles north of Fort Washington, he encamped most of his army at Fort Greenville, where it would winter. On December 23, he led a force north. On Christmas Day, after a two-day, twenty-three-mile march, the soldiers arrived at the site of St. Clair's defeat on the Wabash River's headwaters. Amid the scattered bones of hundreds of dead, they erected Fort Recovery.

Wayne's strategy was working. The chiefs realized that a surprise attack could not succeed against such vigilant, well-trained, and fortified troops. In June, several hundred Indians attacked Fort Recovery but were driven off with heavy losses. They failed even to destroy any of the supply trains shuttling between the forts. All they could do was watch the Americans for any opening and implore the British not only for ever more arms, munitions, and provisions, but also to war with them against the Americans.

Canadian governor Dorchester was in a tough diplomatic and strategic bind. Among his roles was that of Great Father to all the tribes, not just in Canada but across America's Northwest Territory, which the British controlled. That meant supplying them with trade goods and protecting them against their enemies. He believed that another war between Britain and the United States was inevitable, yet he was under orders not to launch a first strike. Wayne's army appeared impervious to the surprise attack that had destroyed two previous American forces. If Wayne succeeded in defeating the Indians, he could then turn against the weak British garrisons across the territory. To forestall that possibility, Dorchester ordered Simcoe to build a fort on the north bank of the Maumee River, just a dozen miles upstream of Lake Erie. The 120 troops that occupied the new fort, Fort Miami, might either deter Wayne's advance or provoke him to attack, while the Indian confederacy remained united and undefeated.

Wayne was astonished to learn that the British had committed such a provocative act as erecting a new fort on American territory. However, it was a lack of supplies rather than Fort Miami that delayed his advance until July 1794. Once again he had his troops build forts at strategic sites along the way, planting Fort Adams on the St. Mary's River and Fort Defiance at the Maumee River rapids. He was now in the heart of the northwestern Indian confederacy. In August he crossed with most of his army to the north bank of the Maumee River and advanced downstream toward a cluster of villages and Fort Miami.

Astride Wayne's advance, Shawnee chief Blue Jacket and hundreds of warriors lay in wait at Fallen Timbers, a tangle of trees uprooted and strewn by a tornado. Firing broke out as the Americans appeared on the morning of August 20. Wayne ordered part of his army forward to pin down the Indians while he sent a column thrashing through the forest to outflank them. After suffering perhaps a score or so of dead and wounded, the Indians broke and ran. The Americans lost thirty-three dead and a hundred wounded.

Wayne followed up that victory by marching his army within a mile of Fort Miami and sending word to Maj. William Campbell to withdraw his garrison. It was not hard for Campbell to calculate the odds against him. He lacked enough troops, supplies, and, above all, protection for a prolonged siege. Fort Miami was a hastily erected log palisade. Once the American cannons were emplaced within range, they could blast sections of his wall to splinters within an hour or so. Nonetheless, Campbell sent a message back to Wayne that he was under orders to stand firm at all costs.

In that eyeball to eyeball standoff, Wayne blinked first. He ordered his army to withdraw. The British considered Wayne's withdrawal from the gates of Fort Miami nothing short of a miracle. Col. de Peyster marveled that Wayne had retreated "at a time when it would appear he had effectively accomplished his chief object, and defeated the Indians perfectly, and had the whole country at his command."[5]

What explains "Mad" Anthony's decision? His nickname was a misnomer. There was nothing mad about his method of war: careful calculation and then relentless advance within the confines of his orders. And his orders stated clearly that he was to do nothing that might provoke a war with Britain. He had hoped to bluff Campbell into abandoning that post, but Campbell called it. A lack of supplies forced Wayne to backtrack all the way to Fort Recovery, where he and his men sat tight during the long winter. But Wayne did not despair. Time was clearly on the Americans' side.

The Indians in each village had many months to sit around their council fires and mull their fate. In the spring they could either open negotiations or face Wayne's army marching against them. They had fought valiantly for three years and won two brilliant victories. But, with Anthony Wayne, they faced an enemy who could not have been more different than the inept generals Josiah Harmar and Arthur St. Clair, who had earlier led armies against them. Wayne was methodical in his advance and fierce in his attack. He appeared to be unstoppable. The tribes had no choice but to negotiate for the best deal they could get.

It was nearly another year after the Battle of Fallen Timbers before the latest peace was imposed on the frontier. The Treaty of Greenville was signed by Wayne, Little Turtle, Blue Jacket, and other chiefs on August 3, 1795. This treaty merely confirmed the boundaries of five previous treaties. That boundary ran from the Cuyahoga River mouth on Lake Erie to its headwaters, then westward to Fort Recovery, and southeast until it hit the Ohio River at the Kentucky River mouth on the south bank. East and south of that line was most of today's Ohio and a sliver of southeastern Indiana. Every inch of the ceded land would go to restless American speculators, farmers, and entrepreneurs. The Treaty of Greenville departed from earlier treaties in what the Indians gave up beyond that boundary. In Indian territory, the United States could fortify sixteen strategic points and enjoy the unimpeded right of way to and from those posts. And, thanks to another treaty that would soon be negotiated, the Americans would eventually be able to finally occupy the entire Northwest Territory.

14

The Jay Treaty

J ohn Jay embarked for London on May 12, 1794, the same day that a thirty-
day trade embargo with Britain expired and was not renewed.[1] Just what he
was supposed to accomplish in London had been debated in the weeks leading up to May 6, when he was issued his final instructions.

As usual, Hamilton took the lead in making policy. He instructed Jay to convince the British to pay full compensation for their confiscations of slaves during
the War for Independence and of American vessels and cargoes more recently;
withdraw from all their forts in America's Northwest Territory; agree to a trade
treaty based on reciprocity and neutrality laws based on "free ships, free goods";
and cut off all military supplies to the Indians. Jay should sign no trade treaty with
Britain that sacrificed American trade with France. In return, he would agree to
American payments for pre-1775 debts owed to British creditors and would not
allow ship prizes to be sold in the United States. Hamilton let Jay go with a final
warning: "It will be better to do nothing than to do anything which will not stand
the test of the severest scrutiny and especially which may be construed into the
relinquishment of a substantial right or interest."[2]

Had John Jay obeyed that last instruction, he would have saved the
Washington administration and the Federalist Party a severe political drubbing.
Nonetheless, John Jay certainly had an impressive résumé to qualify him for that
vital mission. He was forty-eight years old when he embarked for London after
nearly three decades of public service. Few people in government had filled more
crucial posts or contributed more to nurturing the new republic. After graduating

from King's College in New York, Jay began a career in law that was increasingly influenced by the worsening conflicts with Britain. He joined New York's Committee of Correspondence and was elected to the First and Second Continental Congresses of 1774 and 1775. In 1777 he was a delegate to the convention that drafted New York's constitution. He was elected the president of Congress on December 10, 1778, and served in that post until September 27, 1779, when he was named America's minister to Spain, where he worked hard to get more military aid to the United States. After the war, he returned to his law practice in New York. In 1784, Congress appointed him the secretary of foreign affairs; he served in that post until 1789. That year he joined Alexander Hamilton and James Madison in penning the essays that became known as the Federalist Papers, which so brilliantly explained and justified the Constitution; he contributed five of the eighty-five essays. Like Hamilton, he hated slavery; he sponsored resolutions in 1777 and 1785 that called for abolition. In 1789 Washington named him the first chief justice of the U.S. Supreme Court. As if these duties were not challenging enough, the president also asked him to serve as the secretary of state until Jefferson could return from Paris on March 22, 1790.

Jay's diplomatic strategy with Foreign Secretary Grenville and other British officials was to "strive to accommodate rather than dispute; and if that plan should fail, decent and firm representations must conclude the business of my mission." Meanwhile, he encouraged the president and his secretaries to ensure that America's military buildup continue so that he could benefit from that shadow looming larger behind him.[3]

Jay's mission began well enough after he set foot in London on June 14, 1794. He was cordially received by George III on July 2. His first substantive meeting with Grenville took place on July 11. Grenville was not merely polite but also friendly; he promised to do what he could to make rapid progress toward an agreement. From then it took about four months to negotiate and sign a treaty.[4]

Jay did not have a strong hand to play. America had no army or navy to speak of, just a few tattered, battered regiments far away on the Ohio Valley frontier and a few gunboats rotting at anchor in eastern ports. Although laws had been passed calling for a navy and army buildup, Congress had appropriated only enough to lay the keels of three frigates, and none to raise more troops.

Yet militarily Britain could not immediately muster overwhelming power against the United States. The incomparable Royal Navy was scattered on missions around the globe, while its "red line" was just as thinly dispersed. The war with France was not going well for the British. An armada had briefly taken France's key Mediterranean naval base of Toulon for several months in the autumn of 1793 before being driven off by a plan devised and led by a young major named Napoleon Bonaparte. A British expedition to Flanders was defeated at Tourcoing and forced to evacuate. Britain's allies were faring no better. The French trounced the Austrians at Fleurus in June, while the Prussians and Spanish prepared to leave the war altogether. The only bright spots were in the Caribbean, where British expeditions took St. Lucia, Grenada, Martinique, and Saint-Domingue, although at a terrible cost: about 35,000 British soldiers and sailors died in the West Indies from 1793 to 1798.[5] Every British life lost and every pound sterling expended was one less that could be wielded against the United States.

For Jay, the real diplomatic challenge was not the vast disparity in military power between the two countries but their disparity of interests. The proper nature of America's relations with Britain was the crucible of foreign policy debates in the United States during that era. In stark contrast, America was a peripheral rather than core concern of Britain during that generation of persistent threats looming from just across the channel in France. The fact that Britain's ties with the United States were a distraction rather than priority bolstered Whitehall's already daunting negotiating edge.

Jay's position was further undercut during the negotiations when a report from Hammond reached Grenville on September 30, 1794. The United States would not join the League of Armed Neutrality, which Russia, Denmark, and Sweden had formed in April 1793. Sweden's minister in London had given Charles Pinckney, the American minister, a copy of the treaty and invited the United States to join. After debate within the cabinet, Secretary of State Edmund Randolph politely declined the offer. Hamilton had revealed that policy during one of his free-ranging talks with Hammond. Whether this had any significant effect on Grenville's diplomatic strategy has been debated ever since.[6]

If all those limitations on American power were not burdensome enough, Jay faced a master of diplomacy across the negotiating table. Yet Grenville suffered his own obstacles—as foreign secretary he no more made policy than his American counterpart. The cabinet was nearly as split on what to do about the United States as America's Congress was over what to do about Britain. Although the ministers were of one mind on the issue of war with America, they differed over just how far they were willing to go to preserve the peace. Grenville and Prime Minister William Pitt were relatively conciliatory, while Henry Dundas, the secretary for home affairs, led the hard-line faction. The cabinet finally forged a consensus on the northwest posts, debts, trade with Britain's West Indian colonies, seizure of ships and sailors, and neutrality, of which the last issue was most important. Grenville was to make it clear that American neutrality was essential; any

American favoritism toward France, especially the opening of ports to French privateers, would provoke war.

That worry was the easiest for Jay to soothe. The president had already issued his Neutrality Proclamation and intended to adhere strictly to it no matter how much the Republicans badgered him to do otherwise. The West Indian trade issue was the toughest to resolve. Jay and Grenville finally broke the long, bitter deadlock when the hard-liners grudgingly agreed to allow an opening of West Indian ports in return for limiting the size of American ships sailing there to no more than seventy tons.

Jay then addressed the issue of Britain's seizure of American merchant ships and cargoes. He submitted to Grenville a petition by forty American sea captains who called for compensation for the financial losses and cruel treatment they had suffered at British hands. Here Jay scored a minor victory. Although Grenville refused to submit British naval policy to a treaty's restrictions, Whitehall did address the problem with its Order in Council on August 6. Henceforth the time limit on appeals by those who claimed damages would be lifted, while the seizure of grain shipments to France would be suspended.

Nearly as important was the thorny issue of the British impressment of American sailors. Grenville was gentle in his response. It was certainly not the king's will for Americans to be mistakenly impressed. However, the U.S. government could mitigate the problem if it simply required all sailors sailing on American vessels to carry documents proving their citizenship.[7]

Jay's most morally troubling instruction was to gain compensation for the slaves freed and spirited away by the British during the war. He pressed that point the least. As a founding member and former president of New York's Manumission Society, he suffered a conflict between his personal morality and the political demands of America's slave-owning caste. He must have sighed with relief when Grenville told him that point was nonnegotiable.

Having gotten nothing in writing, Jay submitted on August 6 a draft treaty to Grenville that included all the points of his instructions. It took Grenville several weeks to forge a consensus for a response. On August 30 the foreign minister submitted his counterdemands. If the United States promptly paid its debts, the British would withdraw from the posts in June 1796. The ports of Britain and the United States would be open to each other's goods and ships on the most favored nation status. American vessels would be allowed to trade with Britain's West Indian colonies, but only if those vessels weighed less than seventy tons. The frontier would be redrawn to give Britain a foothold on the upper Mississippi River. The United States would compensate British owners of ships captured by French privateers in American waters. A joint commission of Britons and Americans would examine and rule on any compensation appeals by American shipowners and merchants.[8]

Jay was quick to respond. He countered Grenville's demands point by point in letters on September 1 and 4. He objected most strongly to the demand to redraw the frontier. To Jay's immense relief, Grenville eventually dropped that demand. The American diplomat argued that if British merchants could trade freely with the Indians in the United States, then Americans should enjoy the same right in Canada. Grenville conceded that as well; Americans could trade anywhere within Canada except those lands dominated by the Hudson's Bay Company.[9]

Jay gave Grenville a revised draft on September 30. It included tenets that forbade either side from using Indian allies against the other in war, forging political ties with the other's Indians, and supplying them in their wars against the other government. He also called for demilitarizing the Great Lakes and frontier. As for neutral rights, Britain would accept America's principle of "free ships, free goods" and strike foodstuffs, raw materials, and naval stores from its list of forbidden goods. Joint compensation and boundary commissions would include two Americans and two Britons, with the nationality of a fifth member determined by lot. Of that Grenville would agree only to the commissions, and only then if there were three rather than five members. At that point, Jay gave up trying to pry any more concessions loose and instead worked with Grenville to refine an agreement. Jay and Grenville signed the Treaty of Amity, Commerce, and Navigation on November 19, 1794. The four months of negotiations leading up to that act would prove to be the easy part. Jay would carry back to Philadelphia a political bombshell that would detonate when its fine print became known.[10]

The treaty's journey from signature to ratification was perilous. The official copy took four months just to cross the Atlantic, thanks to storms and prowling French privateers that forced the captain to frequently change course. A leaked version made it over much sooner. Philadelphia's newspapers published what was purported to be a text of the treaty on February 2, 1795, and other newspapers across the country swiftly printed their own versions. That ignited a political firestorm as a range of interested parties protested that Jay had caved in to the British on the vital issues. The most vociferous opponents were merchants, shipowners, and slaveholders.

Washington called for patience until he could review the official text. Congress adjourned on March 4, just five days before the treaty reached the president's desk. Politically, it was a good thing that the nation's senators and representatives had dispersed to their faraway homes. Washington and his men were appalled—the treaty was as disappointing as had been reported. The cabinet could only hope that those senators who had protested the treaty's pirated version most vehemently would cool off during their sojourns at home and return to Philadelphia with open minds.

Instead, when Washington sent the treaty to the Senate on June 8, 1795, the opponents had enjoyed five months of rallying against it. The opening assault came with the first of fourteen essays that appeared in Philadelphia's *Independent Gazetteer* from March to June 1795. The author of the essay, titled "Letters of Franklin," is unknown and had nothing to do philosophically or literally with Benjamin Franklin, who had died four years earlier. The series was largely a tirade against those who would better ties with Britain and a paean to an alliance with America's sister republic France. Hamilton countered by writing thirty-eight essays under the alias "Camillus."[11]

When the Senate took up debate of the treaty on June 8, it was composed of twenty Federalists and ten Republicans. If party lines held firm, the treaty would be ratified. But tenets of the treaty offended Republicans and Federalists alike. Merchant and shipowning interests in the Federalist Party protested all the treaty's trade measures, especially the seventy-ton limit on trade with the West Indies and the prohibition on reexporting goods bought in the West Indies. Deficit hawks and manufacturers decried the twelve-year tariff ceilings that limited revenues and protection. Slave owners shrilly denounced Jay for conceding their "right" for compensation for their "property" "stolen" by the British.

It was not clear whether Washington could muster enough votes to pass the treaty. Even if he could, ratification might prove to be a Pyrrhic victory. The bitterness of the losers on such crucial issues might well tear the nascent country apart.

The parties largely held together on a series of votes that addressed aspects of the treaty. The Federalists defeated proposals that would have postponed the treaty for debate, amended it to compensate aggrieved slave owners, and completely renegotiated it. The most controversial Federalist tactical victory was keeping the treaty's text secret until after ratification. Republicans sidestepped that requirement by leaking the text to their leading newspaper, now the *Philadelphia Aurora* after the *Gazette's* demise. Meanwhile, Hamilton and Rufus King, who led the Federalists in the Senate, worked feverishly behind the scenes to obtain as many firm commitments to the treaty as possible.

Having overcome all those challenges, Washington and his cabinet were confident that they had enough votes for ratification. The president gave King the nod to put the treaty to a vote. The Senate ratified the Jay Treaty by a strict party-line vote of 20 to 10 on June 28, 1795.

Despite the victory, Washington did not want to appear too eager to sign the ratification. While he was biding his time, news arrived that made him and others wonder whether he should not shelve the treaty altogether. The latest shift in Britain's Orders in Council was issued on April 25. The Royal Navy and privateers were authorized to seize any vessels carrying grain to France, a move that appeared to violate the spirit and ambiguous letter of the Jay Treaty. Once again the United States was shortchanged on Britain's priority list of national interests. The confiscation policy was designed to at once deplete the grain warehouses of France and fill those of Britain.

Washington asked Randolph's advice on what to do. The secretary of state replied on July 12 that the United States should pocket the treaty and reopen negotiations for a better deal with Britain. On July 22 the president informed his secretary of state that he agreed with that advice and told him to pass the message to George Hammond, the British minister.[12]

Then, solely by chance, a stunning revelation about Edmund Randolph emerged that forced Washington to ratify the treaty after all. A British warship captured a French vessel carrying Dispatch Number 10 from Jean Antoine Joseph Fauchet, the outgoing French minister, to his foreign ministry. The British captain ordered his men to spread all sail for London. Pitt and his cabinet gleefully read the dispatch then posted it with instructions to the British minister in Philadelphia.[13]

Hammond eagerly shared the dispatch with Treasury Secretary Oliver Wolcott on July 28. Wolcott conferred with War Secretary Timothy Pickering and Attorney General William Bradford. They agreed that the president had to be informed at once. Pickering fired off a letter to Mt. Vernon urging Washington to hasten back to Philadelphia as soon as possible "for a special reason which can be communicated to you only in person."[14]

The president arrived in Philadelphia on August 11. Not knowing that Randolph was the object of Pickering's urgent message, Washington was conferring with the secretary of state when the war secretary appeared. "That man is a traitor," Pickering darkly proclaimed as he pointed to Randolph. Perhaps suspecting what might be coming, Randolph asked and received permission to be excused. The proof arrived later that day with Wolcott and the dispatch.[15]

In a long report on political conditions within the United States, Fauchet revealed that Randolph had spoken of imposing a military dictatorship on the United States and to that end had solicited money from the French minister. He wrote, "This was undoubtedly what Mr. Randolph meant in telling me that under the pretext of giving energy to the government it was intended to introduce absolute power and to mislead the President in paths which would conduct him to unpopularity." The previous year's Whiskey Rebellion was to have been the excuse for amassing dictatorial powers. Randolph planned to use that crisis "to magnify the danger" of the rebels with "the design of uniting themselves with England, to alarm the citizens for the fate of the constitution, whilst in reality the revolution threatened only the ministers." Randolph would have marched the fifteen thousand troops raised to put down the Whiskey Rebellion against the government. He would have been able to bring off his coup because of his "influence . . . over the mind of the President." As for asking for funds, Randolph did so when "he called upon me with a countenance expressive of much anxiety and made the overtures." Although Randolph was the only cabinet secretary who appeared both corrupt and treasonous, Fauchet harshly criticized Hamilton, who "has made of a whole nation a stock-jobbing, speculative, selfish people." He had nothing but praise for all Republicans other than Randolph.[16]

As if the evidence was not outrageous enough for Washington, Randolph had further provoked the president's ire with a circular letter he had sent on July 21 to America's ministers abroad. He condemned the Jay Treaty and expressed his hope that the president would not ratify it but would instead send an envoy to London for a new round of negotiations.

Washington conferred a cabinet meeting the next day and announced that he would ratify the treaty. He then presented the dispatch to Randolph and demanded an explanation. Randolph asked to explain himself in writing, was excused, and resigned later that day. The president needed a new secretary of state but was frustrated in finding one. Four men turned down the offer before War Secretary Timothy Pickering agreed to run both posts until Washington could find a replacement for either. When James McHenry agreed to be war secretary, Pickering became the official secretary of state on December 10, 1795.

Meanwhile, Randolph retired to his plantation to write his "Vindication." He received some aid from Fauchet, who signed an affidavit that exonerated the former secretary of corruption charges. Fauchet's replacement, Pierre Adet, released further information from various dispatches that showed Randolph in a better light. Randolph's "Vindication" helped neither him nor his fellow Republicans as he revealed a web of backroom financial and political deals. In all, Randolph was more a dupe and fellow traveler than an outright traitor. Fauchet described him as "undoubtedly an excellent man, very much a partisan of our revolution, but I believe him to be a weak character; it is very easy to penetrate his secrets once you get him agitated; besides which I do not give him mine except when I want him to know them."[17] The Randolph scandal played to the worst fears and smears of

Federalists that the Republicans could not be trusted; either they were dupes of French revolutionary agents and interests or outright traitors.

With undoubtedly very troubled feelings, Washington signed the treaty on August 14, but the president then followed Hamilton's advice that he send the treaty to Rufus King in London. King would exchange it with Whitehall only after the Council in Order was rescinded. This would boost the minister's power and save time if the British agreed.[18]

The reaction to the Jay Treaty's ratification was severe. In cities and towns across the nation, Democratic Societies marched through the streets and burned copies of the treaty and effigies of Jay in central squares and commons. A mob in Boston destroyed a British vessel that was believed to have preyed on American merchant ships. At one point, a group of Republicans led by Edward Livingston publicly threatened Hamilton. Hamilton responded in his typical manner by challenging to fight each of them in turn. They backed off.

Meanwhile, the treaty went through the final steps to become law. Ratifications were exchanged in London on November 19, 1795, and the treaty was proclaimed to be in effect on February 29, 1796.

Washington's battles over the treaty were far from over. While reports of the mobs were disturbing enough, the president still had to convince Congress to appropriate money to fulfill America's duties under the treaty. Half a million dollars was a lot of money back then, and that was the amount the United States needed to contribute to the commission that would decide the fate of vessels and cargoes seized by Britain's warships and privateers.

Congress reconvened in December after a long recess lasting from late summer. While a majority in the Senate would most likely vote for the money, the House vote was at best uncertain. James Madison was determined to wield Congress's power of the purse to financially starve the Jay Treaty to death. His rival leader in the House was Theodore Sedgwick of Massachusetts. Sedgwick reported to the administration that the treaty was so unpopular across party lines that he could not guarantee a majority.

Washington set aside that controversy for the time being. It was not until February 29, 1796, that he finally declared the treaty to be in effect, and the following day he submitted it to Congress. But no appropriation request accompanied it.

Recognizing that they had the upper hand, the Republicans tried to make the most of it. On March 2 Edward Livingston proposed a resolution that demanded the administration submit to the House all documents concerning the Jay Treaty. The proposal initiated a battle over whether the president's compliance would somehow violate the Constitution's separation of powers and reveal secret information.

Madison modified the resolution on March 7 by leaving it up to the president to decide which papers to withhold. The resolution died by a vote of 37 of 47. Many Republicans had voted against Madison's version because it ceded Congress's constitutional power of oversight. Livingston's unconditional resolution, which strongly asserted constitutional power, carried by a vote of 62 to 37 on March 25.

For five days Washington and his cabinet debated. On March 30 he sent word of his refusal to the House, arguing that the Constitution empowers the president to make and the Senate to ratify treaties, but says nothing about the House. A majority in the House resolved on April 7 that each house of Congress had both the power and the duty to investigate problems and appropriate money. The president and his supporters stonewalled, invoking what would become known as "executive privilege." Although that concept cannot be found in the Constitution, they argued that it was among the executive branch's "implied powers." Further complicating the debate over the Jay Treaty was the arrival of the Pinckney Treaty. Hamilton urged the administration not to link the two for fear Congress would reject them both. But Washington and his cabinet decided on a trade. The administration held out to Republicans the promise of the Senate's ratification of the popular Pinckney Treaty in return for appropriations for the Jay Treaty.[19] As Republicans mulled what they regarded as a Faustian pact, the British helped rescue the administration from its politically and constitutionally precarious position. A key Federalist argument for the Jay Treaty from the moment Washington had laid it before the Senate the previous year was that the failure to ratify and fulfill it would mean war. Whitehall had decided on just that course on January 14, 1796, and had sent instructions to Phineas Bond, the chargé d'affaires in Philadelphia, to make that clear. Bond informed Pickering, and the administration rendered that warning public.[20]

A stirring speech by Federalist Fisher Ames may have tipped the delicate balance in favor of appropriations. John Adams, who witnessed the performance from the gallery, reported that there was hardly a dry eye among either the representatives or the spectators. The House voted 51 to 48 for appropriations on April 30, 1796.[21]

An arbitration commission was set up to oversee the collection of American debts to British creditors. The United States eventually settled those claims by paying out 600,000 pounds sterling in 1802. Meanwhile, the British evacuated the northwest posts in June 1796.[22]

Although the Jay Treaty helped assuage animosities on an array of problems, one that it had sidestepped continued to fester. Britain faced a dilemma. The Royal Navy was its first line of offense and defense. The number of new sailors recruited or kidnapped by press gangs was not keeping up with the number of new ships commissioned and crew losses from disease, discharge, and desertion, so the admiralty issued a new order. Warships would not stop, search, and seize merchant vessels just for their cargoes but for "British" deserters as well.

As a result, American shipowners had another complaint against the British. In response to the Washington administration's protests, Whitehall cited its dubious interpretations of international law. Although a future president would take the United States to war over the issue, Washington, his cabinet, and a majority in Congress did not then think impressment was worth fighting for. Instead, on May 28, 1796, Washington signed a law whereby the federal government would issue passports to sailors if they could prove their citizenship. The trouble was that in those days the sort of documents that could prove citizenship, such as baptismal records, were not readily available, if they existed at all. Many legitimate American sailors went without a certificate and thus were vulnerable to impressment. Moreover, a large proportion of the sailors were foreigners from a range of nationalities. Nonetheless, Pickering instructed Rufus King that henceforth the United States would no longer tolerate any impressment of native or naturalized American citizens, nor non-British foreigners sailing on American ships. King duly informed Grenville.[23]

For years, Grenville had been urging the Americans to set up such a program. Now he changed his tune and protested the policy on two grounds. First, British subjects could easily obtain false papers. Second, Whitehall denied that a Briton lost his native nationality when he took on another; thus naturalized American citizens with British origins were fair game. The new passport program would barely dent the number of sailors kidnapped off American vessels, with ultimately tragic results.[24]

15

The Pinckney Treaty

The diplomatic mission Jefferson had sent William Short on proved to be fruitless.[1] Short reached Madrid on February 1, 1793, the same day that France declared war on Britain, although word of the declaration did not reach Spain for several weeks. A communication lag also followed France's declaration of war against Spain on March 7. Spain officially declared war against France on March 23.

The subsequent alliance between Britain and Spain on May 25, 1793, affected relations between the United States and Spain in two areas. The most immediate was trade. The United States sold much more to Spain than it bought. Twelve percent of American exports went to Spain, whereas only 2 percent of Spain's exports were sold in the United States. If trade were completely cut off between the two countries, the United States would suffer more.[2]

Before the alliance, it was the Spanish who had complained about their trade deficit with the United States, which they blamed on America's discriminatory policies. Hamilton had carefully composed the tariff and tonnage duties in the 1789 and 1790 trade laws to favor American ships and goods. Madrid retaliated in 1792 with a law that mirrored the U.S. laws. But even then the Spanish supported the Americans and defied the British by upholding the "free ships, free goods" principle.

All this changed after Spain allied with Britain. When London authorized warships and privateers to prey on neutral ships carrying "contraband" to French ports, Madrid issued similar orders. The first publicized incident arising from these orders occurred on August 18, 1793, when a Spanish warship captured an American merchant vessel, locked the crew in irons, and sailed on to Corunna. There the vessel was condemned and sold, and the crew languished in prison for another half year. Word somehow got to William Short and William Carmichael, the chargés d'affaires in Madrid, who protested the vessel's seizure and the crew's mistreatment. Foreign Minister Diego de Gardoqui eventually ordered the crew of the American vessel, along with two other ships and their men, which the Spanish had seized and sailed to Cadiz, released. But scores of other American ships would eventually be taken into Spanish ports in Europe and the Caribbean. To add salt to these economic and diplomatic wounds, the Spanish complained that the United States was allowing French privateers to use American ports to attack Spanish shipping.[3]

The other change in American relations with Spain seemed even more important but proved to be a mirage. America's strategy of trying to play off Britain and Spain against each other had appeared to evaporate once the two countries became allies. This, at least, was the discouraging view from Philadelphia. The Spanish did not see it that way. After having dismissed any notion of talks for months, Gardoqui finally summoned Carmichael and Short in November 1793. At an appropriate moment in a long discussion, he revealed a diplomatic bombshell: King Charles IV wanted an alliance with the United States in return for concessions on the Mississippi and boundary.

Word that the United States had sent John Jay to negotiate a treaty with Britain had set off alarm bells in Madrid. The Spanish feared that if the Americans signed a beneficial treaty with the British, they could concentrate their power against Spain. The Spanish were well aware of French minister Genêt's machinations to recruit a frontier army to attack Louisiana. Although Genêt was long gone, rumors of enraged American frontiersmen mobilizing to descend the Mississippi and capture New Orleans or slog through the swamps of northeastern Florida and take St. Augustine continued to swirl. If the Spanish did not act fast, they could end up losing the Floridas and even Louisiana.

Short fired off a long letter to Jefferson in which he explained the opportunity and urged the secretary of state to seize it decisively. But the letter reached Jefferson after he had resigned. His successor, Edmund Randolph, apparently overlooked the letter. With ever-more impatience, Short and Carmichael awaited instructions. The only word they received were separate letters approving the sickly Carmichael's request to be recalled for health reasons and Short's appointment as minister.[4]

The Spanish once more took the initiative, this time through Manuel de Godoy, the latest foreign minister. Godoy, who had risen from being a lowly army officer to foreign minister by being the queen's lover, dispatched instructions on July 26, 1794, to Spain's chargés d'affaires in Philadelphia, José de Jáudenes y Nebot and José Ignacio de Viar. They were to invite President Washington to send a minister to Madrid to negotiate an alliance in exchange for concessions on the Mississippi, the border, and trade.

Complications rendered this potentially crucial message to be among the slowest in diplomatic history. First, the uncertainties of war prevented the dispatch from reaching Jáudenes and Viar until December 8, 1794. Then it took another four months before the envoys could read and act upon the message. Madrid had changed its secret diplomatic code but neglected to inform its envoys in Philadelphia. That was not all that Madrid had neglected. Godoy had not informed Short of his initiative until September 7, 1794, nearly six weeks after he sent it off. Finally, Jáudenes did not like the instructions, so he stripped Godoy's electrifying offer of concessions for an alliance. The version Jáudenes gave Randolph on March 25, 1795, simply asked for talks.

Jáudenes carried the concept of plenipotentiary powers as far as he could even though neither he nor Viar was actually entrusted with such powers. Jáudenes believed he had very good reasons to defer the king's will. The Whiskey Rebellion convinced him that the westerners were ready to detach themselves from the United States, either into independence or outright allegiance to Spain. Jáudenes had been secretly encouraging the Whiskey rebels and traitors such as James Wilkinson and his cabal. He was confident that the king and the minister who was cuckolding him would never seek an alliance nor make any concession if they thought the United States was teetering at the brink of civil war.[5]

In the end, the long delay in delivering an ultimately distorted message from the Spanish to the American government did not matter. Although Washington and his advisers had no interest in an alliance, they were determined to win concessions on the Mississippi, the border, and trade. The previous autumn, Washington had approved Randolph's proposal to send Thomas Pinckney, then serving as America's minister in London, to Madrid. Randolph had sent off letters to Pinckney and Short on November 9, 1794, explaining the former's appointment as minister. Although Pinckney received his instructions on January 13, 1795, it would take him months to finish up his affairs in London so that he could embark.

Thomas Pinckney was a proud member of that wealthy South Carolina plantation clan that contributed so many notable people to America's revolution. Few Americans of that or any other time enjoyed a better formal education. Pinckney graduated from Westminster School, Oxford University, and the Inner Temple, where he received a law degree. In 1772 he returned to South Carolina to start a law practice. Despite or, more likely, because of his education in England, he was a fervent patriot and opposed Britain's policies toward the American colonies. Upon learning of Lexington and Concord, he joined the army and fought until he was wounded at Camden in 1780. After the war he entered politics, was elected to the state legislature, and served as governor from 1787 to 1788. In 1791 Washington offered him a judgeship, which he declined, and then the post of minister to Britain, which he accepted. In all, Pinckney was an excellent diplomat with his keen intelligence, worldliness, legal knowledge, and political skills. In Madrid, he would have a strong diplomatic hand to play, and he would play it for all it was worth.

Spain was not just feeble in the New World. The war against France had been a disaster from which the Spanish were eager to extract themselves. They succeeded in doing so by signing a peace treaty with France at Basel on July 22, 1795. Peace with France might have strengthened Spain against the United States. But the war had financially exhausted Madrid, and there was no incentive to assert power in North America.

Pinckney reached Madrid on June 28, 1795. It took him four months to negotiate a treaty with Godoy. It took a while just to overcome the initial surprise at Spain's request for an alliance. Nothing in Pinckney's instructions suggested that possibility, let alone what to do if an alliance were offered. And that alliance with the United States would be all the more vital for Spain once the British learned of Spain's separate peace with France. Even more importantly, the Spanish feared that the Jay Treaty, whose content was not yet known, represented an alliance between the United States and Britain. The worst nightmare for Madrid would be if both countries warred against Spain.[6]

Pinckney recognized the enormous advantage these Spanish fears gave him. To Randolph, he wrote, "The new position of Spain with respect to England will induce them to come to a decision with us."[7] Pinckney thus took a hard line with the Spanish. He politely dismissed the notion of an alliance while insisting on free navigation down the Mississippi and beyond, the deposit of goods at New Orleans, a border at the 31° latitude, compensation for shipping depredations, and finally most favored nation trade status. For months, Godoy rejected Pinckney's requests before conceding on nearly all of them.

The breakthrough came on October 24, when a thoroughly disgusted Pinckney announced he was going home and demanded his passport. When Godoy met him the next day, he handed him not his passport but a list of concessions. He did insist that the Americans had no "right" of deposit at New Orleans, only the "privilege" for three years, with automatic resumption if another place elsewhere in Louisiana could not be mutually agreed upon. Pinckney and Godoy signed the Treaty of San Lorenzo on October 27, 1795.

When Washington unveiled the Pinckney Treaty to the public, the reaction was as enthusiastic as it had been scathing for the Jay Treaty. The 31st parallel would be the border. Spanish troops would be withdrawn within six months of the treaty's ratification. Americans could descend the Mississippi to the sea and deposit goods duty-free at New Orleans. Trade between the two nations would be founded on most favored nation status. A mixed commission would evaluate appeals for seized ships and cargoes.

The only trouble was a possible legal ambiguity between the Jay and Pinckney Treaties, with the former opening the Mississippi River to American citizens and British subjects alike, while the latter granted the right of descent only to Americans. The Washington administration finessed this by simply interpreting the Jay Treaty as granting the British the right to navigate the American portion of the river; the British would have to cut their own deal to voyage within Spanish territory.

Ratifications were exchanged on April 25, 1796. Then, as was typical, it took Spain's bureaucratic wheels a long time to grind into action. A royal order for Spanish troops to withdraw from posts on what was now American territory was not issued until September 22, 1797. It would be well into 1798 before the posts at Natchez, Nogales, and St. Stephens were turned over to the Americans. But for now, American trade flowed unvexed down the Mississippi River to New Orleans, and often to the Gulf a hundred miles beyond.

16

Fraying Ties with France

The mutual recalling of Edmund Genêt and Gouverneur Morris by Paris and Philadelphia created vacancies that each government had to fill. As a favor to Republicans, Washington nominated James Monroe in May 1794. The Senate approved the nomination on May 27, and he boarded a ship bound for France on June 18.

The National Convention not merely received but celebrated Monroe as its guest on August 14, 1794, and even made him an honorary French citizen. The French adored Monroe because he was a leading Republican, and they associated him with other Francophiles like Jefferson and Madison. The new minister also benefited from an upward spike in French regard for the United States. A French convoy filled with American food dropped anchor in Brest on June 13, thus averting a famine caused by bad weather and too many men drafted into the army.

Monroe's chief mission was to convince the French to repeal their decree of May 9, 1793, which authorized the seizure of American and other neutral ships carrying food to France's enemies. But on April 6, 1794, the Convention had actually rescinded that policy. With this already done, Monroe could bask for a while in the enthusiasm bestowed upon an American Republican in Paris.[1]

Monroe's popularity was a double-edged sword. It bloated not only his ego but also his adherence to the ideology that inspired it, and thus it warped his ability to understand and advance American interests in France. Washington became ever more upset as reports reached him that Monroe appeared to be advancing

Republican and French interests at the expense of the policies of the American president who had sent him there.

And as if that were not irritating enough, the French were once again trying to entangle the United States in an alliance against Britain. In January 1796 Foreign Minister Charles Delacroix began to implement a plan "to take advantage of the ferment that agitates the United States, to make them declare that power against England."[2] Although an alliance was certainly a sensible French goal, the means Delacroix proposed to cultivate American sympathies were simply a reprise of the follies that prompted Washington to eject Genêt, such as meddling in party politics and trying to turn public opinion against the government. And, while mouthing platitudes of republican solidarity, the French were warring against the United States, as their navy and privateers captured scores of American merchant vessels as prizes.

Yet that contradictory policy is somewhat understandable. Like the British, the French had more important things to worry about than the United States. And in France, as in America and Britain, interest groups badgered policymakers to advance themselves, often at the nation's expense. More often than not the result was a contradictory rather than a coherent policy. Finally, starting in May 1796, the French were emboldened by the dazzling victories of a young general named Napoleon Bonaparte, who would eventually capture northern Italy and repel all Austrian attempts to retake that region. Elsewhere French armies staved off allied offensives.

On March 11, 1796, the Directory, the name for France's latest government, issued Monroe an official letter with a list of complaints against the United States. The key points were that the United States had persistently and grossly violated both the alliance and commercial treaties of 1778. Monroe made a lengthy reply, countering each point.[3] The worst French complaint of all was against the Jay Treaty, which Paris interpreted as shifting America's alliance with France to Britain. Monroe's toughest diplomatic challenge was to defend the Jay Treaty, which he had himself opposed. Paris retaliated by issuing on July 2, 1796, a decree that all but declared total war on American commerce.[4]

At the other end of the diplomatic channel, with his low-key approach to diplomacy, Jean Antoine Joseph Fauchet, Genêt's replacement as minister in Philadelphia, had defused some of the Federalists' anger against France provoked by his predecessor's machinations. For sixteen months after his arrival in February 1794, Fauchet was largely seen as both politically and socially constructive. Then came the revelations of the Fauchet dispatch that the British captured and glee-fully turned over to the Washington administration in August 1795. It appeared that Fauchet and Genêt had differed only in style; both had intrigued against the American government. Indeed, Fauchet was the more successful, having been able to corrupt Secretary of State Randolph against Washington's administration.

Most Americans could be forgiven if they suspected that Pierre Adet, who replaced Fauchet, would be as much of an intriguer as his predecessors. He did not disappoint. First, there was his personality—he poorly disguised his distaste for America and Americans and his regret at having set foot in the United States. He heatedly protested Washington's ratification of the Jay Treaty as a violation of the 1778 commercial treaty between the United States and France.

Then came the revelations that Adet had authorized a French general to embark on an intelligence-gathering mission down the Ohio and Mississippi Valleys from Pittsburgh to New Orleans. Victor Collot was the former governor of Guadeloupe who had been captured by the British and released on parole in the United States. Adet asked the general to pay special attention to secession sentiments among the westerners. Collot embarked on his journey in March 1796 and returned, laden with reports, by ship from New Orleans in December 1796. He stepped ashore into a diplomatic crisis. Although Collot could be praised for all the intelligence he gathered, the gregarious man violated a crucial element of spy craft—he spilled the beans. As the Frenchman traveled, he spoke openly with as many prominent westerners as possible about separating from the United States and forming an independent country under French protection.[5]

Word of Collot's mission reached Treasury Secretary Oliver Wolcott, who shared it with the president and his cabinet. Although Collot had a two-month head start, Washington had War Secretary McHenry fire off a letter to Arthur St. Clair, the Northwest Territory governor, instructing him to seize Collot and his papers and forward them under guard to Philadelphia. But Collot was already far beyond St. Clair's reach.

Given all the suspicions and affronts on either side of the Atlantic, French respect for James Monroe was virtually the last diplomatic fig leaf obscuring the broken relationship. They lauded Monroe as a true American republican while castigating the Washington administration and the Federalists as British sycophants. That fig leaf was torn away when Monroe was recalled.

Monroe's very popularity discredited him in the minds of Washington and other Federalists. They increasingly feared that he was playing a double game, pretending to advance the administration's policies while covertly undercutting them. Wolcott, Pickering, and McHenry presented Washington with a joint declaration on July 2, 1796, that Monroe should be replaced and cited his ill-disguised opposition to the Jay Treaty as the most compelling reason.[6]

The declaration was the last straw for Washington, and he began tapping shoulders for a replacement. Being assigned to Paris in the midst of revolution, war, and terror was not considered the choicest of foreign posts. John Marshall politely declined. Charles Pinckney reluctantly succumbed to the president's pressure, but there was a catch. The Directory refused to receive Pinckney when he arrived in November 1797. After three months of fruitless waiting, he withdrew to the American mission in The Hague to await instructions. He would be a long time waiting.[7]

17

The Farewell Address

Washington's second term as president was even more challenging than his first, although ultimately it was successful. He skillfully avoided any commitment to France that might have dragged the United States into war against Britain and its allies. Treaties with Britain and Spain resolved some of the grievances with those countries. After agonizing over years of defeat, the president tapped a general who routed the northwest Indians and brought peace to the Ohio Valley. Yet he suffered his share of setbacks and disappointments. Most notably to his deep regret, he could do nothing to heal worsening national divisions and quell the rise of the Republican Party and the Democratic Societies, although he was able to suppress the tax revolt they inspired known as the Whiskey Rebellion.

In his Farewell Address, George Washington left enduring axioms that expressed the art of American power in the early republic. James Madison had first written a draft of the speech for Washington when he had planned to retire in 1792. Four years later Alexander Hamilton dramatically revised it. The speech publicly appeared on September 19, 1796, nearly a half year before he actually left office.[1]

Washington summed up the nation's achievements during the first eight years under the Constitution and then addressed current and future challenges. Peace and prosperity fed each other and in turn depended on other vital attitudes and behaviors. Unity was essential. He warned his countrymen strongly against "the baneful effects of the spirit of party," especially "those of the popular form," which are government's "worst enemy." He called on his countrymen to be Americans first and above all: "The name of American, which belongs to you in your national capacity, must always exalt the just pride of patriotism more than any appellation derived from local discrimination." Patriotism is not simply a matter of sentiment but is also grounded in self-interest: "Every portion of our country finds the most commanding motives for carefully guarding and observing the union of the whole."

Washington and his fellow Federalists firmly believed in peace and prosperity through both economic and military strength. A crucial role of government was to nurture the economy by investing in projects that spurred development while avoiding needless debt. The United States also needed an army and navy strong enough to deter foreign aggression. Those public duties, in turn, depended on each citizen doing his part. The only duty always demanded of citizens was to pay their part, for "to have revenue there must be taxes."

Adept diplomacy was yet another key ingredient of promoting prosperity and peace. The United States must "observe good faith and justice toward all nations. Cultivate peace and harmony with all. . . . In the execution of such a plan nothing is more essential than that permanent, inveterate antipathies against particular nations and passionate attachments for others should be excluded, and that in place of them just and amicable feelings toward all should be cultivated."

Interests governed the behavior of states and individuals alike. That meant that other nations would often try to strengthen themselves at America's expense. Thus Americans had to be on guard against "foreign influence" that sought to "tamper with domestic factions" and "practice the arts of seduction to mislead public opinion." The danger posed by those intrigues varied with the power of the state that practiced them. The worst scenario was "the attachment of a small or weak toward a great and powerful nation" that "dooms the former to be the satellite of the latter." Americans must "be constantly awake" against that threat "since history and experience prove that foreign influence is one of the most baneful foes of republican government."

The essence of Washington's approach to American interests, power, and foreign policy boiled down to this: "The Great Rule of Conduct for us, in regard to foreign nations, is in extending our commercial relations to have as little political connection as possible." The reason for that axiom was that "Europe has a set of primary interests which to us have none or a very remote relations." Thus "it must be unwise in us to implicate ourselves by artificial ties in the ordinary vicissitudes of her politics or the ordinary combinations and collisions of her friendships or enmities. Our detached and distant situation invites and enables us to pursue a different course." But, if the worst should happen and the United States had to go to war to protect vital interests, then "we should safely trust to temporary alliances for extraordinary emergencies." By following these axioms, "the period is not far off when . . . belligerent nations . . . will not lightly hazard giving us provocation; when we may choose peace or war, as our interest, guided by justice."

The Farewell Address distilled the essence of the art of power in the early republic. And no one was more skilled at expressing and practicing that art than Alexander Hamilton.

PART 3
Adams, 1797–1800

I will never send another minister to France without assurances that he will be received, respected, and honored as the representative of a great, free, powerful, and independent nation.

JOHN ADAMS

A public ship carries no protection but her flag. I do not expect to succeed in a contest with you, but I will die at my quarters before a man shall be taken from this ship.

CAPT. THOMAS TINGEY, U.S. NAVY

No! No! Not a sixpence!

CHARLES PINCKNEY

The French captain tells me I have caused a war with France. If so I am glad of it, for I detest things being done by half measures.

CAPT. THOMAS TRUXTON, U.S. NAVY

Wherever the government appears in arms it ought to appear like a Hercules.

ALEXANDER HAMILTON

18

John Adams and American Power

John Adams had rather humble origins for someone who would later be condemned by his political foes as a would-be aristocrat with monarchial pretensions.[1] He was born into a farming family in Braintree, Massachusetts, about a dozen miles around the bay from Boston. As a young man, he was content to work the land, but his father had higher ambitions for him. Recognizing his son's keen intelligence, he sent him off to Harvard with the misplaced hope that he would become a minister. By the time Adams entered college, he felt a greater calling to stand before a bench rather than behind a pulpit. That choice disappointed his controlling father and further cooled the then distant relationship between them. It also reinforced a naturally cantankerous independent streak in Adams.

Adams was an early American radical. The first flames of his radicalism were kindled in 1760 by James Otis's fiery oratory against British abuses in Boston's statehouse and in taverns. Five years later, Adams penned his own paean to liberty with his "Dissertation on the Feudal and Canon Law," which condemned British policies by comparing them with other tyrannical regimes throughout history. Adams became so influential in dissident circles that Governor Francis Bernard tried to co-opt him by asking him to serve as the colony's advocate general in the admiralty court. Adams refused to compromise his principles. Instead he championed his respect both for the law and liberty by helping defend the British soldiers accused of murder for firing into a crowd of rioters in December 1770, a tragedy known as the Boston massacre; he was able to convince a jury to acquit all but two. He was elected to the General Court, where he was an out-spoken critic of British policy.

Adams was among the five elected to represent Massachusetts at the First Continental Congress in 1774. For the next quarter century he served almost continuously in public life. In 1775 he was reelected to the Second Continental Congress, which would sit nearly continuously until the Americans won independence. Impressed by his "Thoughts on Government," which was published in early 1776, Congress chose him to be on the five-man committee charged with drafting the Declaration of Independence.

No American in the early republic had more prolonged or varied diplomatic experiences than John Adams, who spent most of the years from 1778 to 1788 overseas. During the Revolution, he served in Paris, The Hague, and London, and he was America's first minister to the Netherlands from 1782 to 1785 and to Britain from 1785 to 1788. Like Jefferson, he was abroad during the 1787 Convention and thus played no direct role in crafting the Constitution. Shortly after he returned home in 1788, he was elected vice president of the United States. He dutifully endured eight years in that understudy role in an administration in which his counsel was rarely solicited.

John Adams will never be ranked among the most beloved of the Founders. His friends and foes alike have described him as vain, pompous, irritable, irritating, opinionated, pontificating, petty, vengeful, and haughty.[2] Unlike many of his type, he at least recognized his faults even if he could do little to curb them: "Oh! that I could war out of my mind every mean and base affection, conquer my natural Pride and Self Conceit; expect no more deference from my fellows than I deserve, acquire that meekness and humility, which are the sure marks and Characters of a great and generous soul."[3] But, try as he might, he was incapable of doing so.

Adam could eviscerate himself for his faults, but he was thin-skinned when anyone else did so. His mercurial personality affected his politics and policies. Jefferson recalled that Adams "never acted on any system, but was always governed by the feeling of the moment."[4] Franklin noted, "Adams was an honest man, often a wise one, but sometimes wholly out of his senses."[5] He was no natural politician. A friend of his admitted that he "can't dance, drink, game, flatter, promise, dress, swear with gentlemen and small talk and flirt with ladies."[6]

Adams, however, made up for his shortcomings with a keen sense of public service: "I feel guilty—I feel as if I ought not to saunter and loyter and triffle away this Time—I feel as if I ought to be employed for the Benefitt of my fellow Men, in some Way or other."[7] But an even more powerful motivation was his belief that he was destined for greatness and thus had to do all he could to secure his place in history.

No Founder other than Hamilton wrote more about political philosophy.[8] Adams's major works alone—"Thoughts on Government," "A Defense of the Constitution of the Government of the United States of America," and "Discourses on Davila"—weigh down a book shelf. Alas, his prose, like his oratory, could be long-winded, dense, and meandering. He tended to summarize the views of others in a rather repetitious way. None of his tomes will ever be ranked among the classics of political philosophy. Yet he was wise enough to know his limits. For reasons of both style and politics, he urged Jefferson to pen the Declaration of Independence rather than himself.

The essence of his philosophy was an attempt to institutionalize that elusive balance between liberty and order. Every man was plagued by an incessant war between his reason and passions in which the latter more often than not had the edge. Man should always strive to realize virtue and the public good. That was possible only if his baser instincts and emotions could be repressed. To assist that, governments were instituted among men. Like other conservatives, Adams feared a mob more than a dictator, and thus he favored a stronger rather than weaker government. Yet he was never the aristocrat, let alone the monarchist, that his enemies smeared him as being.

Perhaps no president has spent more time trying to run the country from his home. Adams passed about half of his four years in his farm house in Quincy, Massachusetts. He claimed to be able to manage the nation's affairs just as effectively there as in Philadelphia: "The secretaries of State, Treasury, War, Navy, and the Attorney General transmit to me daily by the post all the business of consequence, and nothing is done without my advice and direction."[9]

For most of his presidency, Adams occupied the central position in the political and ideological tug-of-war between Republicans and Federalists. His nods in rhetoric or policy one way or the other could decisively tilt the power balance. He led what became known as the "moderate" Federalist faction, as opposed to Alexander Hamilton's so-called "high" faction. It helped that Adams enjoyed Federalist majorities throughout his presidency, with 22 to 10 in the Senate and 57 to 49 in the House during the Fifth Congress, and 22 to 10 and 60 to 46 in the Sixth Congress.[10]

Considering this overwhelming advantage, what is remarkable is that Adams did not do more as president. His want of political skills may seem puzzling, given that no early American was more experienced as a diplomat. Yet experience does not necessarily equal ability or expertise. The straight-talking Yankee farmer with a puritan mind was out of his depth in the Old World capitals with their intricate webs of politics, amorality, and etiquette. His want of patience, perspective, and humor made him as ill-fitted for diplomacy as he was for politics.

His decade overseas, however, did provide him with one essential attribute that served him well as president. He developed a very clear outlook on the United States and its place in the world. He believed that America should emulate the Great Powers in rooting its foreign policy in national interests rather than in ideals. He agreed with Washington, Hamilton, and the other Federalists that the best principle to guide the nation's interests was to trade with all and permanently ally with none. That, however, did not mean that all relationships were equally important. Here again, he championed the Federalist view that, given America's economic dependence on Britain, the United States would have to devote special attention to nurturing that relationship.

Few presidents have delegated more of their authority to their cabinets than John Adams. In doing so, he essentially yielded the political field to Hamilton, whom he detested. Hamilton may have returned to his New York law practice, but he remained the ever hovering ghost at the policy table. Three men of his faction—Oliver Wolcott as Treasury Secretary, James McHenry as War Secretary, and Timothy Pickering as Secretary of State—packed Adams's cabinet and served as Hamilton's mouthpieces and actors. Like a puppet master, Hamilton skillfully manipulated the strings of power in Philadelphia, mostly through his dominant faction within the Federalist Party but also by influencing public opinion through his powerful essays.

In retaining those personalities from Washington's administration, Adams hoped to reassure the Federalist Party and the public that continuity rather than change would characterize his presidency. He preserved the status quo, however, at a harsh political cost. Wolcott, McHenry, and Pinckney continually put their loyalty to Hamilton first. Like Washington, Adams sought to include a token Republican among his advisers, in this case Charles Lee as the attorney general. Outgunned in his own cabinet, Adams found himself almost continuously compromising or outright losing on most policy debates.

Finally, there was the vice president. Like John Adams before him, Thomas Jefferson's talents would be wasted in that position. During his four years as president, Adams only once asked Jefferson for help on foreign policy. Two days before his inaugural, he tried to talk Jefferson into leading a peace commission to France. After Jefferson refused, Adams "never after that said one word to me on the subject or ever consulted me as to any measure."[11] Yet Jefferson's isolation within the Adams administration was not without its political advantages. Aside from presiding over the Senate, a vice president had plenty of time on his hands. Jefferson put that time to good use advancing the Republican Party's political agenda.

19

The XYZ Affair

Trying to avert war with France would be the greatest challenge for John Adams and the core of his foreign policies.[1] When he took power, France had been at war with most of Europe for five grueling years. Recently a dim light had appeared at the end of that long dark tunnel. Prussia dropped out of the alliance against France in 1795. Spain had converted from an enemy into a neutral in 1795 and then into a French ally in 1796. A French army had over-run the Netherlands and transformed it into a puppet regime called the Batavian Republic. In 1796 Napoleon Bonaparte had led an army into northern Italy and defeated a succession of Austrian armies, and he was now negotiating a peace treaty that would transform northwestern Italy into the Cisalpine Republic con-trolled by France.

Nonetheless Paris faced enormous challenges in turning these successes into a decisive victory that would end the war. The French lacked the sea power for a crushing blow against their nemesis, Britain. The British in turn dominated the seas, had picked off the French colonies of Guadeloupe and Martinique, and were extending their influence over Saint-Domingue. But there were limits to British power as well. Although Britain ruled the waves, it lacked enough troops for a successful invasion of France.

The Directory, France's five-man executive, paid little heed to the United States, which posed no military threat to France. It thus made no sense either to try to deter America from being an enemy or to entice it into being an ally. America's importance lay in its trade. Ideally, the Directory would prevent

American merchants from trading with Britain and other enemies while diverting those shipments to French ports. The trouble was that Britain's fleet had chased most of France's warships from the seas and bottled them up in harbor.

The only way the French could fight back was to loosen small naval squadrons and privateers to prey on enemy and neutral shipping alike. With a decree issued on May 9, 1793, Paris had first authorized privateers to capture American and other vessels if their hulls were carrying contraband or war supplies to Britain. From then until Waterloo, twenty-two years later, that policy would shift markedly. Before Bonaparte took power, the swings in policy reflected a dynamic between rival French political factions and France's fortunes on the battlefield. The initial decree was repealed only two weeks later on May 23, revived on May 28, repealed again on July 1, revived on July 27, repealed on March 24, 1794, revived with amendments on November 18, 1794, repealed on January 2, 1795, restored on July 2, 1796, and then reinforced on March 2, 1797, so that not just any contraband goods, but any ship without a notarized list of its crew was fair game. The March 2 decree repudiated Article 23 of the 1778 Treaty of Amity and Commerce, which upheld the principle of "free ships, free goods." The French justified doing so as retaliation against the Jay Treaty.[2]

The result was a devastating French war against American shipping known as the Quasi-War. By the end of 1797, French warships and privateers had captured at least three hundred of America's five thousand vessels involved in international trade, or 6 percent. Exports fell from $67 million to $51 million, and imports from $81 million to $75 million from the previous year. In the Caribbean, American trade dropped from $24 million to $19 million. Insurance rates for ship voyages soared from 6 percent in spring 1796 to 15 to 25 percent that fall. Rates rose steadily with the losses to peak at 30 to 33 percent in 1798. By the time the Quasi-War ended in September 1801, the French had captured 2,309 vessels. Although the French government was legally obligated to pay owners for the confiscation of their vessels, it did so with a depreciated paper currency, although the value never reached the abysmal depths of America's own currency during its Revolution.[3]

The seemingly inexplicable policy seesaw was not the only reason Americans found French diplomacy baffling. George Washington wrote War Secretary McHenry that "the conduct of the French government is so much beyond calculation and so unaccountable upon any principle of justice or even the sort of policy which is familiar to plain understanding that I shall not now puzzle my brains in attempting to develop their motives to it."[4]

To settle the conflict with France, Adams sought to send to Paris a bipartisan diplomatic team with two Federalists and a prominent Republican. As has been seen, his first choice as the Republican commissioner was none other than Thomas Jefferson. The two men had not seen each other for years before they met just two days before the inaugural. They had no sooner exchanged salutations when Adams asked Jefferson to head the peace commission that he intended to send to France.

Jefferson politely refused, citing as an excuse his need as vice president to stay in the United States. Adams then said James Madison was his second choice. Jefferson agreed to ask Madison on Adams's behalf but in fact had no intention of letting his political partner go. Within days he told Adams that Madison was not interested. Jefferson and his Republican Party feared a trap whereby they would be blamed if the diplomacy failed or would have to share the glory if it succeeded.

The Republican refusal to participate shook Alexander Hamilton's support for the mission. He had favored the notion of a commission only if it were bipartisan. He had advocated adding a prominent Republican, not to share the blame if it failed, but to better its odds of success. He thought a delegation composed of a Republican who admired the French Revolution and two Federalist skeptics could be a creative and dynamic diplomatic team. He also pointed out that Republican participation would "meet them on their own ground and disarm them of the argument that all has not been done which might have been done towards preserving peace."[5]

The Republicans unfairly smeared Hamilton as implacably anti-French and determined to war against France. Actually Hamilton admired both the French and France, even if he was disturbed by the revolution's atrocities and aggression. He wanted to preserve a strict formal American neutrality in the war between France and Britain. He emphasized forging better diplomatic ties with Britain for practical rather than sentimental reasons. With America dependent on Britain for most of its trade, it would be folly to sever ties with that country. There simply were no inexpensive, good quality substitutes for nearly all British manufactured goods. The attacks by Britain and France alike on American shipping enraged Hamilton, but for now the United States was too economically and militarily weak to retaliate. So Hamilton was of one mind with Adams in seeking peace with France.

As Adams explained it, France "is at war with us, but we are not at war with France."[6] His job was to convince the French to stop warring against the United States. That would be no easy matter. French policies seemed designed to weaken, ravage, and humiliate the United States. On March 24 word reached Philadelphia that the Directory had refused to receive Charles Pinckney, whom Washington had dispatched the previous year to replace James Monroe. Apparently the directors were miffed that someone who was openly skeptical of the French Revolution would take the place of an unabashed admirer. So Pinckney was in Amsterdam cooling his heels and awaiting instructions.

That diplomatic insult atop years of depredations against American shipping spurred Adams to do whatever he could to ensure reciprocal diplomatic and economic relations with France. The day after he learned of Pinckney's rejection, Adams called for a special session of Congress to meet from May 15. He and his cabinet agreed that a military buildup should accompany any eventual negotiations with the French. On April 8 War Secretary McHenry submitted a plan that would boost the army, navy, and port defenses.

Adams explained his intentions in a speech before a joint session of Congress on May 16, 1797. He promised to "convince France and the world that we are not a degraded people, humiliated under a colonial spirit of fear and a sense of inferiority, fitted to be the miserable instruments of foreign influence . . . regardless of national honor, character, and interest." He would do so by avoiding getting drawn into the maelstrom of European power politics; instead he would manipulate that shifting imbalance to advance American interests.[7]

Federalists cheered and Republicans jeered the president's message. Both parties interpreted his words as meaning he would tilt toward Britain to pressure France to yield to American demands. Federalists thought that was the only sensible policy given America's military and economic weaknesses. Republicans believed an alliance with the hated British and war with the beloved French was inevitable. The Senate, dominated by Federalists, resolved on May 23 to endorse the president's policy. The House, in which the Federalists' edge was lighter, offered on June 2 a resolution that emphasized seeking peace over confronting France.

The next step was to determine who would negotiate with the Directory. Despite, or more accurately, because of, the Directory's rejection of Pinckney, Adams was determined that he would be among the three. Francis Dana, a friend and chief justice of Massachusetts's Supreme Court, turned down Adams's request, but the next two men he asked agreed to go.

Of the three, John Marshall is the best known today.[8] The man who a half dozen years later would establish the Supreme Court as an equal branch of government never finished college. Yet through tutors and his own diligent studies, he educated himself in the classics and modern political philosophy. When war broke out with Britain, he joined the army and served nearly until the war's end. During those years, he spent much of his downtime studying law. After independence was won, he passed the bar and became a lawyer. He first entered politics as a Virginia assemblyman in 1782.

Today Elbridge Gerry is best known as the inspiration for the term "gerrymandering," or the drawing of political districts to favor one party.[9] His blatant attempt to favor the Republicans would not occur until 1812 and would be a sordid end to an otherwise distinguished political career. He was elected to the Continental Congress, signed both the Declaration of Independence and Articles of Confederation, was a delegate to the Constitutional Convention, served in the House of Representatives, later was elected to two terms as governor of Massachusetts, and served as vice president under James Madison.

Charles Cotesworth Pinckney was a member of one of South Carolina's most prolific political families.[10] Even though, or perhaps because, he earned his law degree at the Middle Temple in London, Pinckney was a fervent patriot. He returned to America to serve without distinction both in South Carolina's government and militia. His rise to brigadier general had everything to do with his family's power rather than any innate military skills. He was a quiet but constructive delegate at the Constitutional Convention. Most importantly, he was a staunch Federalist in the predominately Republican southern states and thus boosted the party's pretensions to having a national presence.

Adams and his cabinet understood that the diplomatic mission stood a better chance of success if it was accompanied by some saber rattling. America's diplomatic clout was inseparable from its economic and military clout. Economically, the United States was still mostly an agrarian country, albeit with large and growing merchant, shipping, and financial sectors. The nation was dependent on Europe and especially British workshops for nearly all manufactured goods.

For better or for worse, a military-industrial complex was many generations in the future. Although the United States did have a large shipbuilding industry that could and would be partly mobilized for war, it lacked other crucial military industries. Lead and gunpowder production was small scale and scattered. There was no mass production of muskets, the standard infantry weapon. Scores of skilled craftsmen working in their homes did annually turn out hundreds of rifles for the nation's hunters. But riflemen were at best auxiliaries to that era's warfare. Although in skilled hands a rifle could be deadly at several hundred yards, compared with a musket's several score yards, it took about twice as long to load and could not mount a bayonet.

Militarily, the United States was a pygmy. The 1794 Naval Act authorized six frigates, but an amendment pared that number to three, and then budget cuts kept those vessels half completed in dry docks. The army's official strength was a mere 3,500 troops, but its actual number was at least a third lower as desertion, disease, and a want of recruits took their toll. Nearly all of the army's poorly trained and equipped soldiers were on the frontier. Although the Republicans celebrated the militia as the nation's first line of defense, historically the citizen-soldiers tended to flee after the first shots.

Led by Hamilton, the Federalists were determined to change all that. As French and British depredations of American shipping worsened, pressure rose on the president and Congress to do something. This allowed the Federalists to push through Congress several laws that bolstered American military power.

Working behind the scenes, Hamilton did what he could to wring enough money from Congress to finish the three frigates and bolster the army. William Smith of South Carolina, who acted as Hamilton's surrogate in the House, introduced on June 5, 1797, ten resolutions designed to build a professional army and navy. Smith's proposal, however, collided with the American tendency to want something for nothing. Although virtually all members of Congress agreed that the United States should boost its military power, few wanted to pay for that by raising taxes. The compromise for a navy bill was to obtain the money by loans and delay an army bill until the next year.

The Naval Act of July 1, 1797, authorized the completion of three of the six frigates begun by the 1794 Naval Act. That important step may have been too little, too late. It would take another year before the frigates *United States* and *Constitution*, with forty-four cannons each, and the thirty-six-gun *Constellation* put to sea. An even bigger problem was that the ships were grossly outnumbered by the scores of warships in France's navy. Yet the odds against the tiny American navy were not as bad as they appeared. The British navy had bottled up most of France's navy in port, while those vessels that were at sea were dispersed and tended to flee rather than fight.

In late July 1797, Marshall and Gerry sailed from Philadelphia and Boston, respectively. Marshall joined Pinckney at The Hague on September 3. They suspected that storms had delayed Gerry's passage. They waited for him until September 18, when they departed for Paris. They reached the French capital on September 26. It was another week before Gerry caught up to them on October 4. They shared a house on the Rue Grenelle, just three blocks from the foreign ministry on Rue de Bac.[11]

The three commissioners met informally and cordially enough with the French minister of foreign affairs, Charles-Maurice de Talleyrand-Périgord, at his home on October 7. What the Americans did not then suspect was that he would demand a very stiff price before he would formally accept their credentials and open negotiations. Typically he did so through intermediaries, who would be code-lettered "W, X, Y, and Z" in the Adams administration's public report of the shakedown.

Jean Conrad Hottinguer, accompanied by Nicholas Hubbard, first conveyed to the Americans the price for a formal meeting with the minister on October 18. Hottinguer was not a foreign ministry official but a Swiss banker whom Talleyrand employed for his private affairs. Hubbard was born in England and was now a Dutch banker. Hottinguer first explained that the Americans had to apologize for what the French felt was the president's aggressive speech of May 16. Then they were to loan 32 million guilders to France and 50,000 pounds sterling to Talleyrand. Thus did Talleyrand seek to rob the Americans of their pride as well as their purse.[12]

The Americans firmly rejected both notions. Two days later, Hottinguer returned, accompanied by another Swiss banker named Pierre Bellamy. The latter explained that Talleyrand was actually a friend of the United States, and it was France's Directory that had to be placated. Bellamy warned that before a treaty could be negotiated, "you must pay money, you must pay a great deal of money." He then presented an elaborate scheme by which the Americans borrowed the money, played international financial markets, and then gave the principle as a loan to France while pocketing the profit.[13]

The obvious scam so outraged Marshall and Pinckney that they were prepared to leave France immediately. Gerry urged them to be patient. They firmly explained to Bellamy that they had no authority to borrow or lend money with anyone. They would, however, be happy to seek such instructions if the French immediately stopped their depredations against American shipping. The Swiss bankers demurred and disappeared for a few days.[14]

France's strategic and diplomatic position vastly improved after word arrived that Napoleon Bonaparte had concluded the Treaty of Campo Formio with Austria on October 17, 1797. Now France could turn its resources toward winning its war with Britain, which involved the Quasi-War with the United States. The two Swiss, accompanied by Lucien Hauteval, made that very point to the Americans and repeated their demands. When asked for an answer, an enraged Pinckney replied, "It is no, no; not a sixpence!"[15]

Gerry sought to break the stalemate with a visit to Talleyrand on October 28. In doing so he played exactly into the foreign minister's hands. Talleyrand was a master at the classic game of divide, isolate, and conquer. After blaming the directors for the shakedown, he suggested that Gerry and one of his colleagues stay in Paris while the other returned to Philadelphia for new instructions.

Gerry informed his colleagues of Talleyrand's idea. After mulling that and other options, the Americans decided on November 11 to write a formal request to Talleyrand for official recognition and negotiations. The foreign minister did not reply. Instead he activated two other agents to pressure the Americans.

Marshall and Gerry were lodging in the home of Reine de Villette, a thirty-two-year-old widow noted for her beauty and charm. Madame Villette was also tied to Talleyrand. One evening when all three Americans had accepted her dinner invitation, she bluntly asked them, "Why will you not lend us money? If you were to make us a loan, all matters will be adjusted. When you were contending your Revolution, we lent you money." Pinckney noted a key difference between the two loans—the Americans merely requested whereas the French demanded.[16]

Then there was Pierre-Augustin Caron de Beaumarchais, the renowned playwright, poet, musician, republican, and friend of the United States. During America's revolution, Beaumarchais had set up a dummy company through which to ship military supplies to the rebels. More recently, he had enriched himself through financial speculations on both sides of the Atlantic. Although Marshall was actually Beaumarchais's lawyer in the United States, he put his country first when he refused his client's request to speak alone with Talleyrand.[17]

Under the Directory's instructions, Talleyrand made yet another attempt to snare the Americans in France's financial speculations. On Christmas Eve, the three astonished Americans turned down a scheme to join with the Bank of Hamburg, buy Dutch bonds at par, and then share the winnings in a loan to France.[18]

Whereas the demands for money were merely insulting, the French were inflicting actual, chronic damage on the United States by ravaging its merchant fleet. The latest outrage occurred on January 18, when the Foreign Ministry issued another decree on neutral shipping. French privateers could now confiscate any ship carrying any British goods. This was a deliberate blow to American shipping because British merchants had been using the neutral U.S. ships to carry their goods. The decree harmed France as much as the United States because American shippers avoided French ports, where their vessels and cargo would be seized if any British goods were found.

Marshall had had enough. He wrote a long memorandum detailing the abuses he and his colleagues had endured since their arrival. Pinckney approved it, but Gerry wished to soften the language. They sent the edited memorandum to the Foreign Ministry on January 31, 1798.[19]

Marshall and Pinckney were not angry at the French only. Gerry's attitude of appeasing rather than confronting the French alienated his colleagues. They protested his private meetings with Talleyrand, his insistence that they yield to French demands, and his refusal that the three demand their passports and leave France. But Marshall and Pinckney had their differences as well, as the former tried to find a way between Pinckney's hard and Gerry's conciliatory lines.

Talleyrand and his agents wielded flattery and party invitations to widen the differences between them. For instance, Gerry and Marshall received invitations to Talleyrand's New Year's ball; Pinckney did not. Gerry went and Marshall, most likely reluctantly, declined.[20]

Talleyrand tried one last ploy against the envoys. As many as 240 Americans lived in Paris at that time; by the Battle of Waterloo this community would swell to more than three hundred people. The attractions of Paris then as now went far beyond it being a center of commerce. A survey in 1797 found 147 merchants, 22 ship captains, 22 land agents, and an array of people from other backgrounds and motivations. It included such famous Americans as the poet Joel Barlow, inventor Robert Fulton, and painter John Vanderlyn. Barlow was the unofficial spokesperson and head of the American community in Paris. Fulmar Skipwith was the official head; he arrived in 1791 to serve in America's diplomatic mission and since 1795 had been the consul general. Talleyrand enlisted Barlow and Skipwith to pressure the envoys to yield to his demands.[21]

Talleyrand did not reply to the American memorandum until late February 1798, then repeated nearly all his demands and accusations. The only change was to demand a treaty promising an additional loan when the war between France and Britain ended. He abruptly abandoned this demand when the three envoys adamantly rejected it.

This was the last straw for two of the Americans. Marshall and Pinckney insisted that there was no point staying in Paris. Although Gerry finally signed a note demanding their passports on April 3, he announced that he would remain in France. The three went their separate ways, with Marshall sailing to the United States, Pinckney and his family sojourning for several weeks in southern France so that his daughter could recover from a severe illness, and Gerry lingering in Paris, where Talleyrand could work his diplomatic magic on him.

Marshall had mixed feelings about leaving France. He quipped to Pinckney that while he was "happy to bid an eternal adieu to Europe . . . & its crimes—Mark I only mean its political crimes, for those of a private nature are really some of those so lovely that it required men of as much virtue & less good temper than you & myself to hate them."[22] Perhaps he had in mind his charming host Madame Villette when he expressed those sentiments.

20

Mustering for War

Two months before he learned of what became known as the XYZ Affair, Adams was already mulling whether to lead the nation to war against France. America faced a worsening economic, military, diplomatic, and political crisis as 1798 dawned. The previous year, French privateers had seized more than three hundred American merchant ships. Insurance rates had soared from about 5 percent to 30 percent for most vessels, and 40 percent for vessels bound to Jamaica. These commercial and financial blows threatened to drag the economy into depression. The nation's merchants, shipowners, and financiers steadily turned the heat up on the president and Congress to act decisively against those depredations.

Adams sought to build a policy consensus within his cabinet. He sent on January 24, 1798, a circular letter to his department heads asking their advice. Attorney General Charles Lee offered the most aggressive policy—he called for withdrawing the commissioners, declaring war, and capturing New Orleans, even though Spain rather than France held title to that territory. Even back then some Americans had trouble distinguishing between adversaries and outright enemies. Had Lee's proposal been adopted, Americans would have found themselves at war with both France and Spain. Hamilton made his views known through his three confederates in the cabinet. He strongly opposed war or even an embargo with France, or an alliance with Britain for now. Instead he sought to strengthen America's negotiating hand through a military buildup. Adams was of two minds on the issue, so for the moment he did nothing.

Then came word on March 4, 1798, that French officials were trying to shake down the American mission. Subsequent dispatches elaborated the insults and obstructions that the three envoys had endured. Adams convened his cabinet on March 13 and asked them whether he should seek a declaration of war. The cabinet split again over the question. This time Lee was opposed. Pickering broke with Hamilton and called for war. McHenry and Wolcott continued to champion Hamilton's position of negotiation through strength. Incensed by the French treatment of his envoys, Adams jumped off the fence and declared that war was an economic and moral imperative. The president heatedly wrote up a war declaration but pocketed it. Instead he gave peace one more chance. On March 19 he submitted a memorandum that countered each of France's bargaining points and announced that limited hostilities already existed.

Not surprisingly, this document provoked a harsh debate between Federalists and Republicans in and beyond Congress. The Republicans introduced three resolutions in the House that opposed warring against France or arming privateers and called for building up coastal defenses. The Federalists managed to prevent a vote on those resolutions. There was a bipartisan agreement, however, that the administration's negotiations with France should be carefully scrutinized. On April 2 the House voted 65 to 27 to request all the appropriate documents. Adams promptly sent the material to Congress the following day but protected the names of Talleyrand's agents with the code letters W, X, Y, and Z for Nicholas Hubbard, Jean Hottinguer, Pierre Bellamy, and Lucien Hauteval. Since Hubbard was referred to only a few times, the conflict was dubbed the XYZ Affair. On April 6 the House voted to print and distribute two thousand copies of the report.[1]

The public revelation of the XYZ Affair was a political bombshell, delighting Federalists and embarrassing Republicans. The result was a dramatic policy shift in both the United States and France toward each other. The scandal enraged most Americans and was the most important force propelling the Adams administration and Congress into the Quasi-War.

The news of the XYZ Affair had the exact opposite effect in Paris. The report's publication there on May 28, 1798, provoked an uproar. Talleyrand disavowed any involvement in the matter. Recognizing their continued need for his diplomatic skills, the directors blandly accepted his explanation. His social and political enemies, however, enjoyed the additional reason to scorn him. Talleyrand had gotten off extremely easy. In that era, being France's foreign minister was a hazardous job. Of the fourteen men who had served in that post from 1791 through 1797, five had been executed, four were in exile, two others had been imprisoned, and only three escaped any harsh treatment. The embarrassing scandal pressured

Talleyrand and the Directory alike to be more conciliatory toward the United States.[2]

As ever-more politicians and other citizens clamored for war, Adams used the surge of support to ask Congress not for a declaration but instead for the military buildup proposed by Hamilton.[3] Adams signed bills on April 27, 1798, that authorized enough money to finish the three frigates and build twelve smaller vessels of twenty-two guns, on April 30 that established a Navy Department, and May 28 that increased the army's authorized strength to ten thousand troops. The army bill was a bluff because Congress would never allocate funds for actually recruiting and sustaining that number of troops.

The Senate approved the president's nomination of Benjamin Stoddert as the nation's first naval secretary on May 18, 1798. By late July the last of the cannons, munitions, and provisions were packed into the three frigates—the *United States*, *Constellation*, and *Constitution*—and they set sail for French prizes and glory.

America's Quasi-War with France was a joint venture of federal, state, and private initiatives. On June 25 Congress passed a law that let merchant ships arm and defend themselves only against French warships and privateers. For now, the Americans turned a blind eye on British depredations of American shipping. The law included instructions on how French prizes should be adjudicated and stipulated that the spoils should be split equally between the ship's owner and crew. Three days later Congress extended these provisions to the American navy, this time with the government taking a cut along with the captain, officers, and crew.

It was soon obvious that building warships would take too long. On June 30 Congress authorized the president to buy twelve vessels from private owners whose price would be paid with bonds bearing 6 percent interest; the government could also accept gifts of vessels that could be converted into warships. Eventually eight vessels were bought and converted: the twenty-three-gun *Ganges*, twenty-four-gun *George Washington*, twenty-gun *Baltimore*, twenty-gun *Montezuma*, twenty-gun *Delaware*, eighteen-gun *Herald*, eighteen-gun *Norfolk*, and thirteen-gun *Augusta*. Prominent citizens of Richmond, Petersburg, Norfolk, and Manchester chipped in to buy, arm, and donate the twenty-gun *Richmond*.[4] These navy ships would be augmented by the ten small coast guard cutters that Hamilton had talked Congress into authorizing in April 1790 so the Treasury Department's Revenue Service could combat smuggling. The trouble was that only two were ready for sea, and even then their operations would continue to be confined to coastal waters. Congress authorized the building of ten new cutters.

Whether a warship was built from scratch or converted from an existing merchant vessel, it faced the same dilemma: how to acquire guns. Foundries in the

United States existed, but the quality was abysmal; their cannons were apt to blow up in the gunners' faces when they overheated. So Treasury Secretary Wolcott gave 45,686 pounds sterling to Baring and Company to purchase British-made cannons. In addition he authorized Rufus King, America's minister to Britain, to spend another six thousand pounds sterling on equal numbers of twenty-four-, eighteen-, twelve-, nine-, six-, and four-pounders for the navy and four thousand pounds sterling on cannons for the army. Of the 370 cannons King purchased from the Woolwich Arsenal, 225 were earmarked for the navy and 145 for the army. When the navy's strength peaked with nine hundred guns in 1800, nearly half were from British foundries. Most of those cannons would still be around to use against the British in the 1812 War.[5]

Congress voted on June 13 for an embargo against France to go into effect on July 1. To that stick, Congress added the carrot that granted the president the discretion to rescind the embargo if France accepted America's demands. But France would not budge, at least for now. President Adams sent word to Congress on June 21 that he had recalled the peace mission and promised that he "will never send another minister to France without assurances that he will be received, respected, and honored as the representative of a great, free, powerful, and independent nation."[6] Then, on July 7 he then signed a law that abrogated all existing treaties between the United States and France. Thus did America rid itself of both 1778 treaties dedicating each country to an alliance and free trade with the other.

The United States came the closest to formally declaring war against France on July 9 when Congress passed and Adams signed a bill that authorized the American navy to seek out and destroy French warships and privateers. The president could also issue letters of marque to privateers to prey on the undeclared enemy.

Congress formally established the Marine Corps on July 11. In doing so, it institutionalized a practice that was as old as the American navy. Since 1775 naval captains had tapped their toughest officers and crew to act as marines. In battle, those men would grab muskets, scramble up the rigging to precarious perches, and try to pick off enemy officers and gunners across the heaving seas and through the billowing gun smoke. When the ships ground against each other, they would leap upon the enemy vessel, madly yelling, swinging cutlasses, and firing pistols. Henceforth, the marines would be organized into detachments, officered, trained, and allocated among the nation's warships. The American marines would soon earn a reputation for being among the world's bravest and most skilled warriors.

The army got a boost on July 16, when Congress authorized the army's expansion from four to sixteen infantry regiments of seven hundred troops each, along with six troops of light dragoons of fifty troopers each. The president could call up to eighty thousand militia to the field. Although that buildup might appear impressive, once again the president and Congress had erected a scarecrow. There was no firm intention to actually appropriate enough money to realize those figures, even though the national budget nearly doubled from $5.8 million in 1796 to $9.3 million in 1800.[7]

That surge provoked another round of the endless debate among Americans over how to pay for government and its array of services. Once again, Hamilton stepped in to ensure that fiscal sanity would accompany military necessity. On July 14 Congress approved a $2 million property tax, and authorized the president to borrow $2 million at no more than 6 percent interest and another $5 million at the best negotiable interest rate. The tax was an especially bold measure. Not only did it violate the ingrained American demand for services without sacrifice, but it fell disproportionately on the nation's two most powerful and often overlapping interest groups—slave owners and the rich. Here Hamilton mingled two of his key moral principles—he hated slavery and believed that the tax burden should be borne by society's wealthiest members. Slave owners paid fifty cents for each of their chattel aged from twelve to fifty, the years when the most profit could wrung from their labor. The average homeowner, whose dwelling cost around two hundred dollars, paid forty cents; those with houses assessed at five hundred dollars paid one dollar fifty.[8]

America's military buildup for its Quasi-War with France was quite a political coup for Adams and the Federalists. With his work done, the president took a well-deserved respite. He fled the capital to his home in Quincy, not just to escape the searing political and summer heat but also to protect the lives of himself and his beloved wife, Abigail; the latest yellow fever epidemic was ravaging Philadelphia and the region. Abigail was sick and would need months to recover. But in devoting himself to his private life, Adams avoided and thus exacerbated the nation's worsening political ills.

21

The War at Home

Word of how the new navy fared against the French would trickle in over the next couple of years. But the results of the incessant partisan warfare at home were immediately known. The battles were not only between the Federalists and the Republicans. The Federalists themselves were split between the so-called high Federalists, led by Hamilton, and the moderate Federalists, who for now backed Adams.

The rhetoric became ever more vicious among the two Federalist factions and the Republicans, with each accusing the others of betraying their country to conspire with foreign powers. Both Federalist factions took to wearing black cockades to differentiate themselves from the Republicans, who had sported French-style blue, white, and red cockades before the XYZ scandal broke and red cockades thereafter. As part of their Fourth of July festivities, Federalists burned effigies of Talleyrand and competed over who could make the most anti-French speeches. When Victor-Marie du Pont appeared in May 1798 to replace Joseph Philippe Letombe as France's minister to the United States, Adams refused to receive him.

The most acrimonious issue between the high and moderate Federalists was over the command of the army. On June 22 Congress empowered the president to commission army officers. Adams began by tapping George Washington as the commanding general. Washington agreed to serve only if he could name his major generals and remain at Mt. Vernon unless a war actually broke out. Adams agreed; he would soon regret doing so.

When Adams received Washington's list, he was outraged to see Alexander Hamilton as the second in command, followed by Henry Knox. That lineup not only jumped Hamilton ahead of Knox on the army's seniority list but put his political archenemy once again in the center of power. He then learned that War Secretary James McHenry had dutifully complied when Hamilton had asked to be called into service. With his typical energy, drive, and skill, Hamilton began to organize the army.[1]

Adams blistered McHenry for calling Hamilton into service without his permission. He insisted that "the power and authority are in the President. I am willing to exert this authority at this moment, and to be responsible for [its] exercise." He went on to lament all the "intrigue in this business with General Washington and me; if I shall ultimately be the dupe of it, I am much mistaken in myself." McHenry offered to resign. Adams declined the chance to replace a Hamilton man with one of his own. Instead he reassured his war secretary: "I have no hard thoughts concerning your conduct in this business and I hope you will make your mind easy concerning it."[2]

Adams was outgunned in the conflict. Pickering, Wolcott, and Stoddert lined up behind McHenry to champion Hamilton. Washington further lent his enormous political and moral weight to his choice. His trump card was the threat to resign if his wish was not honored. That would have been a political disaster for Adams and the country. The president had no choice but to concede, which he did on October 9 with mingled words of resignation and bitterness. When Knox refused to serve under Hamilton, Adams appointed Charles Pinckney in his place. Although the issue was resolved, the animosities lingered.[3]

Despite all the political squabbles, the XYZ Affair and ever-tougher talk backed by the military buildup boosted the popularity of the Adams administration and Federalist Party. Adams and his party squandered that popularity and ultimately destroyed their political power by pushing through and implementing in 1798 a series of laws known as the Alien and Sedition Acts.[4]

The three alien acts dealt only with foreign residents in the United States. The first of those laws, the Naturalization Act of June 18, extended the residence time for foreigners who wanted to become citizens from five to fourteen years. During that time, the would-be American had to register with the government or risk imprisonment. Under the Alien Friends Act of June 25, the president was authorized to arrest and deport without trial anyone he deemed a threat to national security. The Alien Enemies Act of July 6 was a reaction against the excesses of the preceding law. It limited the president's power to arbitrarily arrest and deport aliens to wartime only. Most Republicans protested the June 25 act and supported the July 6 act.

The primary targets of the Alien Acts were the potentially subversive elements among the thirty thousand French then living in the United States. If such agents actually existed, they were but a speck in the population. Most French then living in the United States were refugees from the horrors of the revolution and would hardly have taken kindly to the discovery of one of its cadres in their midst.[5]

Although the Alien Acts stirred debate, the Sedition Act, which Congress passed on July 14, provoked a political firestorm. The Republicans attacked the Sedition Act as an unconstitutional "gag law" designed to rob Americans of the freedom of speech, assembly, and press, and freedom from arbitrary search, seizure, and arrest. The act's most egregious clause forbade "any false, scandalous and malicious writing or writings against the government of the United States, or either house of the Congress of the United States, or the President of the United States, with intent to defame . . . or to bring them . . . into contempt or disrepute."

The Adams administration eventually filed charges against twenty-four people under the Sedition Act; four were found guilty and served time in prison and paid fines. That massive Federalist violation of the Constitution provoked the Republican leadership to go to the other political extreme. The Federalists tried to establish a quasi-dictatorship at home to fight the Quasi-War with France at sea. The Republicans countered with resolves that if carried out would have nullified the Constitution and dissolved the nation into its constituent states.[6]

Working feverishly behind the scenes, Jefferson and Madison mobilized their party in Kentucky and Virginia, respectively penned resolves for each, found sponsors, and convinced each legislature to approve them. John Breckinridge was the political point man for the Kentucky Resolutions of November 16 and December 3. John Taylor mobilized his colleagues to pass the Virginia Resolution of December 24, 1798. Although the wording differed, the arguments and threats of the resolutions were nearly identical. The Constitution was a compact among sovereign states that could freely choose to join or to quit the arrangement. As members, the states could judge which federal laws they would follow and which they would ignore. The Sedition Act violated the Constitution and thus was null and void. Although the Kentucky and Virginia resolves received enthusiastic support in those two Republican strongholds, cooler heads prevailed in the fourteen other state capitals. The assemblies of ten states officially repudiated the resolutions, while the other four were silent. The overwhelming consensus across most of the United States was that two constitutional wrongs did not make a right.

Like the Federalists' Sedition Act, the Jefferson and Madison resolutions turned the Constitution inside out. Nothing in the Constitution discusses, let alone allows, secession. The Supreme Court, not the states, is the final judge of any law's constitutionality. Sovereignty lies in "We the People of the United States," which is expressed through the federal government, not the states. The long-term damage the resolutions inflicted far surpassed the immediate imbroglio. Jefferson's nullification and states rights doctrine would ultimately lead to the secession of the eleven southern states in 1860 and 1861, followed by the horrendous Civil War.

As if the rage between Federalists and Republicans were not hot enough, a tax revolt the following spring threatened to turn violent. John Fries was an auctioneer; father of ten children in Northampton County, Pennsylvania; and fervent Federalist in a predominately Federalist region. Yet he adamantly refused to pay the taxes that the president and Congress had imposed to help fund the Quasi-War. A federal marshal threatened him with arrest. Instead of submitting, he rallied about 150 mostly armed followers on March 6, 1799, marched to the county jail in Bethlehem, and forced the marshal to release eighteen other tax resisters.

The president was preparing to leave for his latest prolonged sojourn at Quincy when he received word of Fries's rebellion. He was inclined to let Pennsylvania governor Thomas Mifflin handle the problem. The president's cavalier attitude toward such a potentially serious crisis appalled Hamilton. The former treasury secretary got his men in the cabinet to convince Adams that to ignore the revolt might encourage others elsewhere. A tough crackdown might deter potential copycats.

So Adams issued a proclamation on March 12 condemning the rebels and calling on Mifflin to mobilize the militia and bring them to justice. He then hurried off to his beloved home. Mifflin, however, was no more eager to confront the rebels than Adams was. He called on the legislature to handle the crisis. Once again, Hamilton intervened. He coaxed his men in the cabinet to talk the president into sending five hundred troops into the region to put down the rebellion. Hamilton insisted that there be no halfway measures: "Wherever the government appears in arms it ought to appear like a Hercules."[7] Hamilton had in mind overwhelming but dignified and restrained force.

Alas, William MacPherson, who was hastily promoted to brigadier general and given the command, was no Hercules. MacPherson enflamed rather than dampened passions with his bullying rhetoric and actions. Sixty prisoners, including Fries, were brought back to Philadelphia. Half were indicted for treason. Fries was found guilty and condemned to death, two others received prison sentences, and others were fined. The brutality with which the troops reasserted order would turn that region to the Republicans in the next election. Then, in Philadelphia, a Federalist mob broke into the shop of the *Aurora*, the leading Republican newspaper, beat William Duane, the publisher, and destroyed his press. To ever-more people across the country, Federalist rule appeared to be synonymous with a brutal, near dictatorship that violated the Constitution with impunity.

Adams consulted his cabinet on whether he should pardon Fries. His cabinet once again took a hard-line stance. This time Adams rejected the cabinet's advice. He issued Fries a pardon on May 21 and released the other convicts from their sentences with pardons on May 23, 1800. This act of clemency could not erase the hard feelings in Northampton County. The Sedition Act arrests and destruction of the *Aurora* caused yet more Federalist voters to decide either to sit home or to vote for the Republicans in the 1800 presidential election and thereafter. For now, however, the Federalists retained their grip on both the White House and Congress. In the midterm elections conducted from late 1798 into early 1799, the Federalists enjoyed commanding majorities in both houses of Congress.

22

The Quasi-Alliance

uring Adams's years as president, the British displayed relative restraint
in their own depredations against American shipping, while hinting at
forging an alliance against the French with the United States. In January
1797 Foreign Secretary William Wyndham, Lord Grenville, instructed Robert
Liston, the British minister in Philadelphia, to assure the Americans that they
could "look to Great Britain as their most natural friend and support."[1] Liston was
to offer British naval protection to American merchant ships against our "common
enemy" if the United States went to war with France. He offered the same assurances to Rufus King, the American minister in London. Interest rather than sentiment demanded a conciliatory stance. With France having briefly won peace on
the Continent, Paris could now concentrate its military and diplomatic guns
against Britain. Thus Britain and America had a common interest in working
against a common enemy.[2]

Britain's conciliatory policy was threatened by a scandal that erupted during
Adams's first year in office. William Blount had fought in the Revolution, had
served in North Carolina's assembly during the 1780s, was a delegate to the
Constitutional Convention, was briefly the governor and then Indian superintendent of the Southwest Territory, and was elected to the Senate from Tennessee
in 1796. Over the years he had wracked up huge debts as a land speculator. To
erase those debts and acquire a vast fortune in land and money, he concocted a
plot to launch a filibustering expedition against Spanish West Florida. His army
would include frontiersman, Creeks, and Cherokees and would be underwritten

with British gold and a British fleet at New Orleans. Robert Liston was Blount's chief backer. It was a dress rehearsal for the conspiracy of Aaron Burr and James Wilkinson a decade later but did not get nearly as far. Blount eventually called off the expedition.[3]

John Adams received incriminating documents about Blount's conspiracy in June 1797. After discussing how to handle the matter with his cabinet, he sent the evidence to Congress on July 3. After four days of debate, the Senate voted 25 to 1 to expel Blount. The House impeached him and sent his case to the Senate. Preoccupied with other important matters, the Senate shelved the case until 1799, when it decided to drop the charges since Blount was no longer a member. Republicans meanwhile castigated Adams for not expelling Liston.

Although other pressing issues soon crowded out the scandal, Blount's conspiracy was a sharp reminder of how much that vast stretch of land between the Appalachian Mountains, Mississippi River, Great Lakes and 31st parallel was a world in itself. Kentucky and Tennessee were now officially states but bore little loyalty and less love toward Philadelphia. The federal government's power to govern the Northwest and Southwest Territories was at best tenuous. Charismatic, ambitious frontier demagogues could gather and lead an army toward their dreams of carving out and ruling empires.

The West was hardly America's only potential Achilles' heel. The nation was straightjacketed on all sides by the great powers and potential enemies of Britain, France, and Spain. Should a war break out with one or more of those empires, immense fleets could scour the seas of American shipping, and agents could stir Indians and turncoats against the American frontier. And while doing that, an enemy could amass an armada of warships and regiments large enough to invade the United States itself. America's leadership had to keep a keen and unblinking eye on the nation's land and sea frontiers, searching for any hint of trouble.

The timing of America's Quasi-War against France could not have been better. The year 1798 was as militarily disastrous for France as the previous year was triumphant. On the Continent, allied armies recaptured most of France's conquests in Germany and Italy. Most decisively for American interests, Vice Adm. Horatio Nelson destroyed much of France's Mediterranean fleet and trapped Napoleon Bonaparte and his army in Egypt at the Battle of the Nile on August 1, 1798.

Washington's Farewell Address had admonished his countrymen to beware of entangling alliances. What he had in mind was the open-ended alliance that the United State had forged with France in 1778 during the war with Britain and that had persisted long after independence was won. Alliances, however, could serve national interests if they were temporary expedients to overcome an immediate and grave threat. In that sense, America and Britain were quasi-allies in their separate wars with France.

America's minister to the Court of St. James, Rufus King, received in early 1798 an intriguing proposal to formalize that alliance. Francisco de Miranda was born in Venezuela, had fought in the American Revolution, and now sought independence for his country from Spanish rule. He lobbied both Whitehall and the American mission for a joint expedition that would expel Spain from the New World and liberate its territories. In return, the United States could take over the Floridas and Louisiana.

Prime Minister William Pitt enthusiastically embraced the scheme: "We should much enjoy operating jointly with the United States in this enterprise."[4] King was just as enthused and sent word to Adams asking whether to proceed. Miranda followed up his talks with King by writing both Adams and Hamilton. Hamilton saw this as a golden opportunity to advance American interests but sought to do so with parallel rather than joint military efforts with Britain. Grenville penned a formal offer of alliance to Adams in June 1798 and sweetened the deal by saying the United States could take Florida and Louisiana while Britain seized Saint-Domingue. In Philadelphia, Liston broached the idea to Secretary of State Pickering in July. Pickering wrote Adams for instructions.[5]

Adams killed the notion. Although he had known of the proposal for months, he had previously declined to comment. The flurry of laws launching the Quasi-War with France and then Abigail's illness had consumed all his energy and attention.[6] There was no want of reasons to dismiss the idea. The least sensible objection was that Hamilton endorsed a version of it. The dispute over whether Hamilton should be second in command was the turning point for Adams. He was now so embittered against Hamilton that he would automatically do or believe the opposite of whatever his rival proposed or endorsed, no matter what the merits were.

But practical concerns surpassed all others. "We are friends with Spain," he reminded Pickering, "If we were enemies would the project be useful to us?"[7] That aside, the United States was already devoting scarce coin to fighting an undeclared war with France. How much more expensive would a war with Spain be? There was certainly no guarantee of victory in either conflict. What if a war-weary Britain bowed out of the struggle? Pickering wrote King, "If Britain yields we shall have the weight of the whole European world against us." That was an exaggeration, but the United States would surely have its hands full if it squared off against France and Spain at once.[8]

Hamilton, as usual, did what he thought was best to advance national interests regardless of what the president desired or demanded. In early 1799 he called Maj. Gen. James Wilkinson, who commanded the frontier army, back to Philadelphia to discuss plans for conquering Louisiana and the Floridas should a war break out with Spain. Washington, however, backed Adams on the issue and discouraged Hamilton from talking about, let alone acting on, the scheme.

Thus did the Americans and British separately fight a common French enemy. At no time were there any negotiations for a formal alliance. Nonetheless, the two navies did coordinate some of their operations. Navy Secretary Stoddert and Vice Adm. George Vandeput, who commanded the Royal Navy's North American fleet, devised a flag signal system to avoid fruitless chases or tragic encounters. Stoddert and Vandeput also worked out a deal whereby American warships could buy provisions from British warships. But that was as far as the quasi-alliance went.

23

The Fate of Saint-Domingue

Complicating Franco-American relations was the fate of Saint-Domingue, which would be known as Haiti in 1804 after it became the second country in the Western Hemisphere to win independence. No colony of any imperial state then produced more wealth for its metropolis than Saint-Domingue did for France. Sugar was white gold for plantation owners wherever it was produced. Saint-Domingue's sugar fields supplied nearly half of the world's supply.

The revolution that broke out in France inevitably spread to the Caribbean. The ideals of liberty, equality, and fraternity not only pitted aristocrats against liberals within the tiny Creole elite, but they also openly turned whites, mulattos, and blacks against one another, and slaves against their masters. Sporadic fighting broke out among the different factions. A prolonged, blood-soaked anarchy devoured Saint-Domingue not long after word arrived that the National Assembly had abolished slavery on February 4, 1794. François Dominique Toussaint Louverture eventually emerged to lead the war for Saint-Domingue's independence.

France's wars with the other European powers, especially Britain, and the worsening chaos and violence in Saint-Domingue offered opportunities for American and other foreign merchants. Few French merchants were willing to risk their ships and cargoes trying to slip past the British blockade and the newly freed slaves, who had an intense hatred of the French. However, neutral vessels packed with desperately needed goods could sail past the blockade and unload safely in Saint-Domingue's ports.

Toussaint Louverture wrote President Adams a letter on November 6, 1798, asking for American recognition of Saint-Domingue's independence. This stirred a debate within the Federalist elite. With varying degrees of enthusiasm or apprehension, the party's leaders concluded that Saint-Domingue's independence would serve American interests since it would at once weaken French power in the New World and enrich American merchants. Hamilton, as usual, was decisive in forging the consensus within the party. He put the key question to Treasury Secretary Wolcott: "Is not the independence of the French Colonies under the guarantee of the United States to be aimed at? If it is, there cannot be too much promptness in opening negotiations for the purpose."[1]

The resulting policy was a delicate political and diplomatic balancing act. The United States would have diplomatic and trade relations with Saint-Domingue without formally endorsing its independence. This policy was codified on February 9, 1799, when Adams signed a bill that empowered him to lift an embargo on American trade with Saint-Domingue if a treaty could be signed guaranteeing protection for American merchants. He then sent Edward Stevens to serve as the consul general to negotiate that treaty with Toussaint Louverture and advise him on how best to achieve independence, even though for now he would receive no official American recognition.

This provoked a barrage of criticisms. Hamilton worried that the policies toward Saint-Domingue and France would become entangled. Of Pickering he asked how "the sending of an agent to Toussaint to encourage the independency of Saint Domingo, and a minister to France to negotiate an accommodation [was] reconcilable to consistency or good faith."[2] The Republicans protested much more than that seeming contradiction. The idea of trading with Saint-Domingue, let alone recognizing its independence, appalled most Republicans. Many leading Republicans were slave owners who were terrified that the abolition of slavery and the race war on Saint-Domingue could spread to America. But for now they were a minority and could only vainly protest Federalist policy.

For the same reasons, Whitehall also opposed Saint-Domingue's outright independence. Prime Minister Pitt sent Thomas Maitland, who had served as an envoy to Toussaint Louverture, to Philadelphia to urge the Adams administration to work with Britain to prevent Saint-Domingue's independence. Soon after arriving on April 2, 1799, Maitland discovered a gap in the British and American positions: "Our policy is to protect, theirs to destroy, the present Colonial System. Our views only go to a partial, theirs to a compleat opening of the Saint Domingo market."[3]

Those differences were soon overcome. On April 20 Maitland, Pickering, and Wolcott reached a gentleman's agreement on Saint-Domingue by which only people from the island with French-issued passports would be permitted to travel on

American or British ships and, if they were diplomats, received by either government. Maitland would return to Saint-Domingue to present the policy to Toussaint Louverture.

Edward Stevens set foot as America's consul general at Cap François on April 18, 1799. After a month he and Maitland scored a diplomatic victory when they convinced Louverture to sign on May 22, an agreement that committed Saint-Domingue to suppress French privateering in its waters and to open Port-au-Prince and Cap François to free trade with America and Britain after August 1, 1799. Louverture refused to accept a British consul, so for now Stevens would handle British as well as American affairs for the island. Upon receiving word of those deals, Adams lifted the trade embargo on Saint-Domingue on June 23, 1799.

The United States did fight one engagement in Saint-Domingue's waters, and it was decisive. On February 28, 1800, Capt. Christopher Perry, commanding the frigate *General Greene*, bombarded the town of Jacmel and the fort with its French garrison. The French fled during the night, and Toussaint Louverture's forces triumphantly surged in the next day. Another American officer found it "impossible to describe . . . the manner in which Louverture expressed his gratitude to Captain Perry."[4]

By August 1800 French resistance in Saint-Domingue had collapsed. That, however, did not end the violence. Toussaint Louverture faced determined rivals for control of the island. The worsening anarchy in Saint-Domingue made it ever more difficult for American merchants to take advantage of the potential trade opened by the treaty. This, however, did not hurt American economic interests. Merchants merely shifted their source for sugar. From 1797 to 1799 American purchase of Cuban sugar rose from $2.8 million to $9 million, whereas purchases from Saint-Domingue plummeted from $8 million to $2.7 million.[5]

Nonetheless, American involvement in Saint-Domingue foreshadowed the importance the Caribbean would have as a theater of American foreign policy in the decades and centuries ahead. As American economic interests grew across the Caribbean basin, the United States would increasingly take sides in conflicts among local factions that were at times backed by other great powers and would often wield gunboat diplomacy to decide the issue.

24

Back Channels

Diplomacy hardly ended after the failure of Marshall, Pinckney, and Gerry's mission to Paris—it just followed different channels. Adams had declared on June 21, 1798, that he would send no more envoys to Paris without a guarantee that they would be treated with respect. But that did not prevent quiet talks between American diplomats already in Europe with their French counterparts.

Talleyrand was in no hurry to resolve the Quasi-War. Although he opposed an all-out war with the United States, he knew French aggression against American shipping had been highly profitable. His strategy was to negotiate in bad faith with the American envoys in order to run out the political clock until the 1800 election, when he hoped that the Republicans would take both the presidency and Congress.

To mask that strategy, he initiated a new round of talks by sending Louis-André Pichon to The Hague to meet with William Vans Murray, America's minister to the Netherlands. The United States was well served by Murray, who was a skilled diplomat and close friend of John Quincy Adams, his predecessor and the president's son. Pichon and Murray had several days of talks beginning on June 26, 1798. Nothing of substance was achieved other than Murray's impression that the French wanted to avoid a war with the United States. He reported that the Americans should capitalize on that fear with a powerful show of strength.[1]

American determination would be conveyed to Paris even sooner. Victor-Marie du Pont, France's consul general to Philadelphia, returned to France in July and explained to Talleyrand that Adams and the Federalists were "hoping the Directory will declare war." He urged Talleyrand not to play into the Americans' hands. France's New World colonies were already imperiled. They might be lost forever if the United States warred successfully against France.[2]

All along Elbridge Gerry had lingered in Paris, hoping that he could strike an elusive deal. His presence pleased Talleyrand, who was grateful for the diplomatic cover for his previous folly. Indeed, Talleyrand so needed Gerry's presence that at one point he refused to return the American's passport when he requested it. Periodically the two would meet, although their talks were inconclusive until July, when Talleyrand made two concessions. France called no more for a loan nor an explanation of Adams's speech and promised to curtail attacks on American shipping.

That was good enough for Gerry, who saw no other serious issues. The next step would be to write these agreements into a formal treaty. But Gerry now had no support from the Adams administration, which viewed him as having betrayed his mission. It would be up to a new team of envoys to negotiate in Paris. Gerry was oblivious to the animosities he had provoked among most leading Federalists. In late July he embarked for Philadelphia to share his success with the president. For that task, Talleyrand gave him a vital going away present. He convinced the Directory to repeal all privateer commissions against the United States on July 31. The Directory made another concession on August 16, when it lifted an embargo on American ships in French ports. The Quasi-War appeared to have quasi-ended.

Then, as now, unsolicited diplomatic initiatives by citizens complicated the president's foreign policy. George Logan, a Philadelphia doctor, Quaker, and outspoken Republican, was determined to prevent an all-out war from erupting between the United States and France. In August 1798 he journeyed to Paris, where he joined the expatriate community of Americans, who were mostly fellow Republicans and Francophiles. With their help and a letter of introduction from French consul general Joseph Philippe Letombe, he met with Talleyrand and Merlin de Douai, the Directory's president. He made an eloquent plea for peace backed with letters with the same arguments from Jefferson, Pennsylvania governor Thomas McKean, and other prominent Republicans.

Once his activism became known, the Federalist press denounced him as a traitor. Federalists bristled at his argument that French aggression only played into their hands and let them drag the country into a war that most Americans did not want. By holding out the hope that a more conciliatory French policy might bring the Francophile Republicans to power, Logan may well have helped that happen. Hamilton was among those who feared a Republican victory in 1800. Upon receiving an intelligence report from Rufus King in London, he wrote, "France will treat, not fight; grant us fair terms and not keep them. . . . Meanwhile our election will occur & bring her friends into power."[3]

Impressed with the Republican message, Talleyrand wrote Pichon that the conflict between the United States and France had resulted from a misunderstanding and fear of the other's motive rather than any genuine clash of national interests. If both sides could only substitute "calmness for passion" and "confidence for suspicion . . . we shall soon agree."[4] He dismissed Murray's suggestion that they find a mediator; they could settle their own problems.

Pichon let Murray read the letter on September 6, 1798, and the next day gave him a copy for his promise not to publish it. Murray promptly sent the letter to Adams. But Talleyrand's conciliatory sentiments were not enough. Murray insisted on a public statement from Paris that henceforth American diplomats would be treated with all the dignity worthy of their position. Talleyrand would not make such a statement publicly or directly. Instead he wrote Pichon that any American diplomats "would be undoubtedly received with the respect due to the representative of a free, independent, and powerful nation."[5] He enclosed a copy of the letter for Pichon to give to Murray. Murray swelled triumphantly at Talleyrand's words. To him it proved the Federalist assertion that France bowed to strength and bullied the weak. The projection of American military power had cowed Paris into a diplomatic retreat: "The United States tore off the mask, and spoke to the world."[6]

Gerry, meanwhile, had returned to Boston. It was not a pleasant homecoming. Federalist ruffians hanged him in effigy, shouted curses, and even placed a miniature guillotine with a blood-smeared blade on his doorstep. Nonplussed, Gerry sent a forty-four page report on his diplomatic efforts to Pickering and hurried to Quincy to meet with Adams.[7] The president stoutly defended his friend against the critics. Gerry had "saved the peace of the nation; for he alone discovered and furnished the evidence that X, Y, and Z were employed by Talleyrand; and he alone brought home the direct, formal, and official assurances upon which the subsequent commission proceeded. . . . Gerry's negotiations were more useful and successful than those of either of his colleagues."[8]

Gerry's report elaborated rather than contradicted the most important points of the reports offered by Pinckney and Marshall. It exacerbated the pressure on Adams to ask for a war declaration during his annual address to Congress, which would come in December. He was willing to make one last effort for peace, but only if he received a French guarantee that the diplomats he sent would be respectfully treated. He could not know that Talleyrand had already made that pledge to Murray, who had forwarded it to the president. As he debated what to do, he received Talleyrand's letter on November 1.

Shortly thereafter Logan returned to Philadelphia. Like Gerry, he was pilloried by Federalists, who resented his interference on both practical and partisan grounds. Secretary of State Pickering gave him the bum's rush. "Sir," he proclaimed with no attempt to hide his contempt, "it is my duty to inform you that the government does not thank you for what you have done."[9] George Washington, who was in Philadelphia to confer with Hamilton over military preparations, was just as disdainful. Much of the loathing for Logan and Gerry was rooted in jealousy and spite; the Republicans had proved more adept at diplomacy than their Federalist counterparts. Washington privately admitted his astonishment that in the art of diplomacy, Logan had bested "gentlemen of the first respectability in our Country, specifically charged under the authority of the government."[10]

Adams returned to Philadelphia in mid-November and solicited his cabinet's views. War Secretary McHenry was eager for war. Navy Secretary Stoddert was not but admitted that for the sake of honor there was no other apparent choice. Treasury Secretary Wolcott and State Secretary Pickering argued that the Quasi-War remained the best policy; no negotiations should proceed unless the French sent an envoy to Philadelphia with a written guarantee that any American diplomats would be treated with respect.[11]

The tension was high when President Adams addressed Congress on December 8, 1798. His top generals, Washington, Hamilton, and Pinckney, stood behind him. Most Federalists must have rejoiced and most Republicans must have feared that the president was about to ask them for a war declaration. To the anger of some and relief of others, Adams did not make the request. With America's navy and privateers at sea, Adams felt he could now negotiate with France from a position of strength. He assured his audience that he was dedicated to a peaceful resolution of the issues with France. To that end he would send another negotiating team to Paris, this time with a promise from the French government that they would be treated respectfully and that the war against American shipping would end. But to further bolster America's bargaining position, he asked Congress to raise an army of thirty thousand troops.[12]

Hamilton found Adams's policy deficient. Although Hamilton did not want war, he felt that Adams had not been tough enough. He shared his perspective with Otis Grey, the House Defense Committee chair. Had Hamilton been president, he would have asked Congress to set a deadline of August 1, 1799, for serious negotiations to begin, or else a war declaration would automatically take effect. The suggestion was not unreasonable. Even with the slow-moving ships of that era, surely talks could have opened well before that date if the French were acting in good faith. Hamilton's second suggestion, however, was a bit more controversial, although just as firmly rooted in reason. He pointed out that since France and Spain were allies, to declare war against one would mean declaring war against both. Since Spain rather than France bordered the United States, any American land offensive should be aimed at conquering the Floridas and Louisiana. He justified that act of aggression "to obviate the mischief of their falling into the hands of an active foreign power" and "as essential to the permanency of the Union."[13]

Adams exploded in anger when he heard of Hamilton's ideas: "This man is stark mad, or I am. He knows nothing of the character, the principles, the feelings, the opinions and prejudices of this nation. If Congress should adopt this system, it would produce an instantaneous insurrection of the whole nation from Georgia to New Hampshire."[14]

In Congress, without a war to debate, the Federalists turned their guns on George Logan, whom they accused of conspiring with France against America. By using Logan as a scapegoat, they were able to push a bill through Congress designed at once to embarrass Republicans and to bolster the government's power to conduct diplomacy. The result was the Logan Act, which Adams signed on January 30, 1799. Henceforth, any American who corresponded with a foreign government with whom the United States was in conflict risked a fine and prison.

The Republicans were down but not out. They had a powerful press and wielded it to shift public opinion in their favor. The central messages were that the French desired peace as much as most Americans and that only misunderstanding and miscommunication prevented a resolution of the issues. To bolster the Republican case, they published the letters, reports, and other documents of Gerry, Logan, and lesser figures involved in resolving the conflict.

One of these figures was Joel Barlow, perhaps the most prominent member of the American community in Paris. Barlow wrote George Washington a long letter analyzing French politics, concluding that the French had no desire for war. Although Washington disdained Barlow as a Republican and an American who preferred to live in Paris, he found his message sensible enough to share it with the president.[15]

Adams received two vital gifts in February 1799 that allowed him to take the next diplomatic step. The French government sent him an explicit written assurance on the issues of the treatment of American diplomats and shipping. And Congress approved the expansion of the army to thirty thousand troops. Adams thus nominated William Vans Murray, the minister to the Netherlands, as the new minister to France. It would take until May for Murray to receive his orders and arrive in Paris.

As usual Adams smacked into a wall of vehement opposition. Pickering, for one, protested at not being consulted on the choice of Murray. Radical Federalists condemned him for preferring to talk rather than fight. Prominent senators led by Theodore Sedgwick threatened to vote against Murray's nomination. Adams threatened to resign if the Senate did not approve his choice.

Adams's cabinet split bitterly over his proposal to reopen negotiations, with Pickering, Wolcott, and McHenry opposed, and Stoddert and Lee in favor. The president was able to overrule the majority because most moderate Federalists supported him, including such heavyweights as Washington, John Marshall, John Jay, Henry Knox, and, with qualifications, Hamilton. A compromise was reached with the Senate whereby two more envoys would join Murray in Paris. On February 25, 1799, Adams nominated Patrick Henry and Chief Justice Oliver Ellsworth. The Senate confirmed all three. Henry was unable to serve, so Adams nominated William Davie in his place; the Senate also confirmed him.

Adams and his cabinet then debated and eventually drafted a treaty that they would submit to the French government. The treaty contained three key points: France must pay indemnities for the depredations of American shipping, American vessels did not have to carry a *role d'equipage* or notarized crew list, and the United States was not bound to recognize France's Caribbean colonies. They then hammered out the exact instructions that would guide the commissioners, finally reaching a consensus on October 15, 1799.

25

The Quasi-War

The agreement to talk was the beginning of the Quasi-War's end.[1] Although the Quasi-War with France is remembered for a few isolated, dramatic ship duels, it mostly involved hundreds of seizures of merchant vessels by navy warships and privateers. Nearly all encounters involved an unarmed or under-armed vessel striking its colors when a more powerful warship fired a shot across its bow.

The most important reason for the paucity of battles was that Britain's navy rather than America's bottled up most French warships in port and picked off many that ventured to sea. The British boasted more than 150 warships of all types whereas the United States had a mere 22. America's navy had no massive ships of the line bristling with fifty or more cannons. Its largest warships were three frigates: the *United States* and *Constitution* with forty-four guns each and the *Constellation* with thirty-six guns. There would eventually be about a score of smaller armed vessels, mostly sloops with a dozen or more guns and schooners with a half dozen or so. But the navy's official ship list obscures the actual range of American naval power. More than a thousand merchant ships were armed to defend themselves and even take French vessels should the captain deem the odds in his favor.

Navy Secretary Stoddert's strategy also made ship-to-ship engagements unlikely. He split the warships under his command between the revenue cutters patrolling home waters and the navy organizing and protecting convoys of merchant vessels to and from the French privateer–infested waters of the West Indies.

144

This strategy may not have won the navy much glory, but it was extremely cost-effective; insurance rates plummeted for ships that sailed with convoys.

Finally, the Directory had reacted to America's war preparations by adapting a policy of restraint. Marine Minister Edme Étienne Borne Desfourneaux sent orders to the fleet to desist attacking American warships, although privateers were still allowed to prey on American merchant vessels. That half measure of bowing to the strong and devouring the weak would have provoked scorn had Americans known of it.

Unfortunately, the French did not convey their policy of restraint to the United States, let alone engage in serious negotiations to resolve the outstanding issues. Nor did the policy last long. Upon hearing of French losses, the Directory promptly declared war on the United States on March 14, 1799. But it was months before news of the declaration reached France's scattered warships.

Despite all those constraints on the "war," the United States did score some wins. Americans celebrated their first victory when word arrived that on July 6, 1798, the sixteen-gun *Delaware* had taken the twelve-gun French schooner, the *Croyable*. The victorious captain's name was Stephen Decatur. His daring and skill in the Quasi-War and later in both the Barbary Pirate War and the War of 1812 made him America's most acclaimed naval officer of that era. The *Croyable* was pressed into American service under the name *Retaliation*. The French recaptured the vessel four months later.

After that dramatic beginning, the Quasi-War drifted into inaction as most French warships sought winter ports in the Caribbean colonies of Guadeloupe and Saint-Domingue or back in France. American warships in search of prey ventured into the Caribbean. The *Constellation*, captained by Thomas Truxton, scored the first American coup of the new year when it captured the thirty-six-gun *Insurgent* after a fierce battle on February 9, 1799. Truxton defiantly concluded his report to Navy Secretary Stoddert, "The French captain tells me I have caused a war with France. If so, I am glad of it, for I detest things being done by halves."[2]

The Quasi-War's last significant battle took place on February 1, 1800, when Truxton's thirty-six-gun *Constellation* inflicted more damage than it suffered in a running fight with the fifty-four-gun *La Vengeance*. Truxton could claim to be the winner because the *La Vengeance* fled. But it was a hollow victory. Although the French suffered four times as many casualties, both ships were so battered that each would barely manage to regain a port for months of repairs.

Despite the rarity of actual battle, the nascent American navy sailed with distinction. Operationally, the navy peaked from December 1798 to April 1799, when, of its twenty-two warships, twenty were at sea at any one time and nineteen were cruising the West Indies. During that time, the navy ships captured nine privateers and recaptured five American vessels. Although the navy's exploits, especially those of the frigates, made the headlines, the Revenue Service's small coast guard cutters actually scored more victories. These nine sloops and schooners captured twenty-six French ships and recaptured ten American merchant vessels. Indeed, America's navy actually outsailed Britain's in the West Indies. Throughout the conflict, the number of American warships in those waters averaged only sixteen, yet they captured eighty-six French privateers, or 5.38 each. Britain's navy, in contrast, averaged eighty ships but took only twenty-nine, or .36 each. Each American warship was fifteen times more successful than its British counterpart. And during the entire two-and-a-half years of conflict, the United States lost only one warship to the French. More than 6,500 prisoners were in America's hands by the war's end.[3]

The fighting was not confined to sea. The marines won honors in September 1800 when fifty leathernecks under Lt. James Middleton were sent ashore from the warships *Merrimack* and *Patapsco* to reinforce Dutch and British troops defending Fort Amsterdam, in Curaçao, from a French expedition. This determined defense forced the French to break off their campaign.

Yet most Americans of that era can be forgiven if they were only vaguely aware that their nation was at war. After all, the actions were limited in scale and number and took place far away on distant seas. Those who bought foreign goods may have noticed a rise in prices. But the only people directly affected by the war were that tiny but rich sliver of the population whose livelihoods depended on international trade, and that group had much to cheer about in 1799. Ship losses plummeted to a third and insurance rates to half their level a year earlier. While American naval operations were an important reason for that, the tendency of merchant vessels to arm themselves and fight back also played vital roles. Nonetheless, the French damaged the United States by confiscating $20 million worth of American ships and cargoes from 1795 to 1799.[4]

What did the United States gain from the Quasi-War? That conflict inspired the birth of what would be the permanent American navy sooner rather than later, and thus the nation was better prepared for the even greater challenge to come—taking on the Royal Navy during the 1812 War. The investment, however, had a nearly immediate payoff for America's economy as the loss of American merchant ships and insurance rates dropped sharply. A congressional committee found that the navy had saved the United States the direct costs of $9.5 million, and the building, launching, and provisioning of the warships further boosted the economy. Perhaps the most important result cannot be counted. Americans regained a bit of self-respect after years of humiliating bullying at the hands of Britain, France, and Spain.

The navy's administration could not have been leaner—Stoddert and seventeen other men operated on a $22,000 budget. Of course, the cost of building or buying and packing ships with cannons, munitions, and crews was exorbitant for the young republic. That shoestring budget did not inhibit Stoddert. On November 23, 1799, he proposed to Adams that the navy be expanded to twenty warships of twenty-four guns, a dozen frigates, and a dozen ships of the line with fifty or more guns. Although he undoubtedly winced at the enormous costs of such a buildup, the president approved the request. Stoddert took his case to Congress. Citing expenses, the legislature cut his plan in half, to six seventy-four-gun ships of the line in a bill passed on February 25, 1799. Then, on the day before Adams left office, in a parting gesture of fiscal parsimony, he signed the Peace Establishment Act, which suspended the construction of the six seventy-fours. Nonetheless, the number of smaller warships kept growing. By late 1799, two schooners, eleven frigates, and nine ships of the line were at various stages of planning or construction. By June 1800 the American navy boasted thirty-two warships.[5] Most importantly the Navy Department and warship captains had gained invaluable experience for fighting the wars that lay ahead.

26

British Depredations and American Honor

As the Quasi-War with France petered out, Republicans were quick to note that British warships were seizing hundreds of American merchant ships and sailors. In principle, they demanded to the Federalists, should not the United States be as tough toward Britain as it was toward France?

The Federalists countered that a range of practical considerations trumped the principle of freedom of the seas and commerce. Britain's policy was two-faced—the Royal Navy protected as well as confiscated American ships. The distinction rested on whether the captain found aboard either British deserters or contraband heading toward French ports. With hundreds of British merchant ships taken annually by the French, Whitehall relaxed the navigation laws to allow American merchants to sell goods in Britain that were officially banned. Finally, with its overwhelming naval power, Britain posed an invasion threat to the United States that France could not then match. Overall, it made sense to tolerate British depredations as long as the benefits outweighed the costs.

It was one thing to shrug helplessly at Britain's confiscation of American merchant ships and sailors. But on November 16, 1798, five British warships stopped a nine-vessel convoy guarded by the American naval sloop, the *Baltimore*. Capt. John Loring, the British flotilla's commander, ordered his marines to search the vessel and examine the crew and had fifty-five men seized on suspicion that they were British citizens. When the *Baltimore*'s captain, Isaac Phillips, protested that the arrests left him without enough hands to man his vessel, Loring released all but five men.

Word of Loring's aggression enraged most Americans. Adams angrily denounced the act to British minister Robert Liston and fired off a letter instructing his minister in London, Rufus King, to protest the incident to Whitehall. Grenville offered a largely conciliatory reply. Although Britain would not rescind its "right" to board and search neutral navy vessels, it would refrain from doing so against American warships as long as friendly relations prevailed between the two countries. Grenville did add that, although Loring should not have made such a demand in the first place, Phillips had after all acquiesced rather than resisted.[1]

The president was determined that no American captain would ever bow again to a foreign captain without a fight. He dismissed Phillips from the service and circulated a stern order to the fleet: "It is the positive command of the president that on no pretence whatever you permit the public vessel of war under your command to be detained or searched, nor any of the officers or men belonging to her, to be taken from her . . . so long as you are in a capacity to repel such outrage on the honor of the American flag."[2]

The message was clear to America's naval captains. Their duty was to defend their vessels and American honor against all odds. The first test of that policy occurred in March 1799 when the British frigate, the *Surprise*, stopped the American brig, the *Ganges*, and its captain demanded that all British sailors be surrendered. Although he was outgunned two to one, the American captain, Thomas Tingey, issued a defiant written reply in capital letters: "A public ship carries no protection but her flag. I do not expect to succeed in a contest with you, but I will die at my quarters before a man shall be taken from this ship."[3] The British ship promptly sailed away. Tingey had courageously scored a triumphant victory against the Royal Navy without a shot being fired.

The Republicans challenged the president's policy toward Britain through a court case. In 1797 the crew of the HMS *Hermione* had mutinied, murdered nearly all the officers, set sail for the United States, and then scattered, with most finding hammocks on American ships. In 1799 the British consul in Charleston, South Carolina, spotted Thomas Nash, one of the mutineers, and asked the local federal court to arrest and extradite him for trial.[4] When the federal court arrested Nash, the Republicans championed him as a hero and organized his defense as Jonathan Robbins, a native of Danbury, Connecticut. Liston asked Adams to look into the case. After examining the evidence, Adams concluded that Nash was lying about his identity and had the court release him into British custody. Nash was eventually hanged.

Even though Nash admitted his true identity in the scaffold's shadow, the Republicans made him a martyr in their pantheon. They introduced a motion in the House of Representatives censuring Adams for his handling of the Nash case. The Adams administration was able to dilute some of that Republican public relations gloss with another case involving the *Hermione* mutiny. When the British asked federal authorities to arrest William Brigstock, Secretary of State Pickering found that he was indeed an American citizen and had the court release him. A resounding vote of 61 to 35 helped defeat the censure motion. Although Adams felt vindicated, he remained bitter at the series of attacks by Republican congressmen and editors.

27

Settling Scores with France

William Vans Murray, the minister in Paris, informed Foreign Minister Talleyrand on May 5, 1799, of Adams's intention to reopen negotiations if he could be guaranteed that France would treat American envoys with respect and seriousness. Talleyrand not only made the guarantee but asked the Marine Minister Desfourneaux to renew his efforts to ensure that any imprisoned American sailors be freed. When that policy proved to be less than rigorously implemented, Talleyrand asked police minister Joseph Fouché on July 7 to ensure that any remaining American sailors be released.

Perhaps no one in history has experienced more political deaths and rebirths than Talleyrand. He had an uncanny ability to judge the health of each regime that ruled France and would jump any political ship that appeared to be sinking with little chance of salvation. One such shift occurred on June 18, 1799, when the National Assembly asserted its power by firing all the directors except Paul François Nicolas Barras. The new Directory accepted Talleyrand's offer to resign on July 13, just five days after he asked the police minister to free the American sailors.

Karl Friedrich Reinhard replaced Talleyrand as foreign minister and promptly reversed his predecessor's conciliatory policy toward the United States. He flexed his nation's diplomatic muscles by pointing to France's alliances with Spain and Holland and insisted that the United States would be overwhelmed if France waged war against it.

This policy of intimidation backfired as it provoked American anger rather than fear. The Adams administration had resolved to launch an all-out war against

151

France if a last attempt to negotiate a settlement failed. The three men Adams chose for his second diplomatic team were as able as his first.

Oliver Ellsworth of Connecticut graduated from the College of New Jersey (Princeton) in 1766, began practicing law in 1771, served in the Continental Congress from 1777 to 1783, was a delegate to the Constitutional Convention, was an author of the 1789 Judiciary Act that created the Supreme Court system, and then was appointed the chief justice in 1796.[1]

William Davie was also a College of New Jersey graduate. After earning his degree, he joined the army in 1777 and fought valiantly for the next five years. He settled in North Carolina and was elected nine times to the State Assembly before being picked as a delegate to the Constitutional Convention. He returned to the Assembly, was appointed major general of the militia in 1794, and was elected governor in 1798.[2]

William Vans Murray did not have as striking a résumé as his colleagues, but he was the only one of them with any diplomatic experience, and he spoke French. He was born and raised in Maryland, earned a law degree at the Middle Temple in London, and then returned to the United States in 1787 to open a practice. His eloquence and intelligence not only won him many cases but also got him elected to Maryland's State Assembly. In 1796 Washington named him the minister to the Netherlands. He served there with distinction until Adams asked him to serve as minister to France in 1798.[3]

Ellsworth and Davie did not sail from Philadelphia until November 3 and set foot in Lisbon twenty-three days later. It was a swift but rough passage that hit Ellsworth especially hard. Even before setting foot on dry land, the two Americans decided to rest up in Lisbon for several weeks to recover before embarking on the second leg of their voyage. In Lisbon they heard news that gave them another reason to sit tight for now. Napoleon Bonaparte and his followers had overthrown the Directory on November 9, 1799, and established a government known as the Consulate. During their sojourn, Ellsworth and Davie hoped to receive a report from Murray on France's political situation and Bonaparte's attitude toward the United States. No word arrived. On December 21 they sailed for the Netherlands and then journeyed overland to Paris, where Murray greeted them on March 2, 1800.

Murray gave them the good news that Bonaparte appeared to be eager for reconciliation with the United States. To that end, he made his first conciliatory gesture little more than a month after he took power. In decrees on December 13 and 19, he rescinded the order that allowed privateers to seize any neutral ship carrying British goods and restored the most favored nation privileges of the 1778 commercial treaty.

News of George Washington's death reached Paris on February 1. As a great admirer of Washington, Bonaparte made three gestures of homage that would further reassure the Americans of his good will. He decreed ten days of mourning, commissioned a bust of Washington to be placed in the Tuileries Palace alongside those of great ancient and French generals, and presided over a commemorative ceremony at the Temple of Mars on February 9.

Bonaparte ordered Talleyrand, whom he had restored as foreign minister, to devise a plan for resolving all outstanding bilateral issues. Talleyrand's subsequent report called for both sides "to dissipate by frank explanations the suspicions that have been reciprocally aroused; to agree on the three treaties of alliance, commerce, and consular establishments; to restore to both sides the enjoyment of their rights, and to find the means of compensation for wrongs done."[4] Finally, Bonaparte decreed on March 27 the creation of a Council of Prizes to which cases could be appealed. This satisfied Americans' and other foreigners' complaints that the local prize courts were arbitrary and corrupt.

So the first consul had made key concessions before the talks even took place. He cordially received the three American commissioners on March 8, 1800, amid a two-day "splendid levee," or grand party, at Mortefontaine, his brother Joseph's chateau about twenty-three miles northeast of Paris. Like virtually everyone else who encountered him, the Americans were starstruck by Napoleon Bonaparte. His charisma was so dazzling that Ellsworth whispered excitedly, "We must make a treaty with this man."[5]

The first consul presented the Americans to their French counterparts: his brother, Joseph; Pierre Louis Roederer; and Charles Pierre Claret de Fleurieu. On April 2 they opened formal talks, during which the Americans presented a draft treaty that the French respectfully received. The American envoys were relieved that there were no vulgar attempts to shake them down for bribes. Yet it would take nearly a half year of tough talks before the two parties could sign a treaty. Although Bonaparte had already made some important concessions, there were still wide gaps to bridge.

The American and French positions had a curious inconsistency that dovetailed with each other. The Americans wanted France to acknowledge the release of the United States from the 1778 treaties and to compensate for the hundreds of ships lost to privateers. The French countered that any abrogation of a treaty had to be mutual. Thus Congress's abrogation on July 7, 1798, was invalid. Yet even if the treaties remained in force, the French depredations against American shipping did not violate them, and thus no compensation was owed.

The Americans replied with powerful rebuttals. First, they claimed that under international law, states enjoyed as much sovereign right to withdraw from as to enter into a treaty. They then argued that the French seizures of American ships violated the letter of the 1778 treaties and thus released the United States from them; Congress's abrogation was a mere formality that acknowledged the treaties as dead letters. Regardless of whether the treaties still bound the two nations, most of the French seizures of American ships violated international law of the sea.

That diplomatic tug-of-war was overshadowed by the latest war. Bonaparte's brief, nearly catastrophic, and ultimately decisive Italian campaign against the Austrians in May and June 1800 solidified both his international and domestic power. Restoring good relations with the United States was on his to-do list when he returned to Paris on July 3. Bonaparte met with the American commissioners at a banquet at Joseph's chateau on July 11. Although he was as cordial as before, he firmly and clearly insisted on two points. First, compensation was potentially due only if the treaties remained in force. Second, he would reject any new treaty unless France received the same benefits that Britain did under the Jay Treaty.

The Americans offered a proposal on July 15 that they maintained was the far-thest they could stretch their instructions. Compensation could be delayed until the Jay Treaty expired in 1803; then the United States could restore to France the trade privileges that it enjoyed under the 1778 commercial treaty. The French diplomats immediately dismissed that proposal. They demanded most-favored-nation status now, not later. They also insisted that they owed no indemnities.

Bonaparte once again tried to cut the Gordian knot by presenting a clear choice to the Americans. On August 11 he sent word that they could either recognize the 1778 treaties and receive some compensation, or sign a new treaty based on most-favored-nation status and do without compensation.

Meanwhile, the Americans learned that an almost entirely symbolic source of unstated bargaining power had disappeared. On February 20, 1800, a coalition of moderate Federalists and Republicans had voted to suspend any more army enlist-ments until the next Congress was convened or a war was declared. Another law, which Adams signed on May 14, 1800, entirely disbanded the provisional army. That army's original rationale had never been terribly strong, since there was virtually no chance that the United States and France would fight a land war against each other. Its value lay in the threat it posed to France's ally Spain, whose adjacent, thinly pop-ulated, and weakly defended territories of Louisiana and the Floridas would have been easy pickings if a war broke out. But that army, which never enlisted more than a fraction of the thirty thousand troops envisioned, was merely an extremely expensive paper tiger that neither Spain nor France took seriously. Bonaparte's suc-cession of conciliatory steps made the army ever more of a farce than a force. After that burden was shed, the military's budget fell from $4 million to $3 million.[6]

It was more than a month before the Americans made an acceptable counteroffer. On September 13 they suggested agreeing to disagree on the issues of the treaties and compensation. For now those could be set aside while other issues were addressed. Each side could simply restore the others ships and cargoes. Trade between the United States and France would enjoy most favored nation status. As for the future, they could agree on mutually binding rules for neutral maritime commerce.

That offer broke the deadlock. Bonaparte gave the go-ahead for both sides to write the terms up into a treaty of twenty articles. The first draft of the Convention of Peace, Commerce, and Navigation, better known as the Convention of Mortefontaine, was finalized on September 27 and signed on September 30, 1800.

The Mortefontaine treaty was the centerpiece of Bonaparte's attempts to rally neutral nations against Britain. Whereas the League of Armed Neutrality with Sweden, Denmark, and Russia fell apart, the treaty with the United States would endure. The importance that the first consul attached to the treaty was reflected in the lavishness of the celebration he threw at Joseph's chateau, where the treaty was signed. More than 180 French and foreign dignitaries attended the party in which the three Americans were the guests of honor. During the banquet, Bonaparte made a speech in which he praised America and the treaty restoring relations between the two nations. He then presented the Americans with small purses of gold Roman coins; he was later amused when they discreetly and politely returned that gift for the sake of propriety. The festivities continued with a concert and two short plays, and concluded with spectacular fireworks.

Davie, arriving in Philadelphia on December 16, carried the treaty back to the United States. Adams submitted the treaty to the Senate four days later. After weeks of acrimonious debate, the Senate rejected the treaty on January 23, 1801, when a vote of 16 to 14 fell short of the two-thirds necessary for ratification. Most of the treaty's opponents were from Adams's own party. Their strongest objection was to Article II, which set aside the issues of the 1778 treaties and compensation. A compromise was reached on February 3 through amendments that rejected Article II and required the treaty to expire after eight years. The revised version was ratified by 22 to 9. Of course, the French would have to approve the changes.

Signing the treaty was easy enough. Enforcing it would prove to be nearly as difficult as negotiating it. The biggest problem with ending the war was technical. It would take months and months to send word to all the warships and privateers cruising the seas to cease and desist from further depredations.

28

The 1800 Election

S igning the Convention of Mortefontaine was John Adams's last significant act as president. Although he lauded the ending of the Quasi-War as his greatest accomplishment, bitterness must have poisoned some of the triumph as he held the document in his hands. He was a lame duck president with only weeks left in office. And he had been defeated as much by his fellow Federalists as by rival Republicans. For years, the high and moderate wings had been locked in an ever more vicious battle for control over the party and over policy. Hamilton's high Federalists had won nearly all the most important battles and, in doing so, had left proud, acerbic John Adams ever more humiliated and enraged.

The final break came in May 1800 during a caucus to decide who the Federalist Party would nominate to run for president. Adams won a consensus on May 3 and selected Charles Pinckney as his running mate. But in those days, the candidate with the second largest number of votes became vice president. So even if Adams won, Pinckney would not automatically win with him. Hamilton conspired not so secretly behind the scenes for the Federalists to rally the electors in each state to vote for Pinckney rather than Adams for president. If his man Pinckney were president, Hamilton would most likely receive a cabinet post and once again determine the nation's fate.

Adams erupted in wrath when he learned of the machinations of not just Hamilton but also his followers in the cabinet. He summoned War Secretary McHenry and denounced Hamilton as "the greatest intriguer in the World—a man devoid of every moral principle—a Bastard, and as much a foreigner as Gallatin. Mr. Jefferson is infinitely a better man." He then turned his rage on McHenry for following Hamilton. McHenry resigned on May 31, 1800.[1] Adams then demanded Pickering's resignation and fired him when he refused. He did allow Wolcott to stay in office even though his allegiance to Hamilton was no secret. He tapped Samuel Dexter, a Massachusetts senator, to be the war secretary and John Marshall to be the secretary of state. The Senate swiftly confirmed both choices, but neither would find much to do in the nine months left in office.

Adams was not mollified by ridding himself of McHenry and Pickering. His greatest nemesis remained at large, conspiring to deny him the presidency. After returning to Quincy in July, Adams spoke out even most forcefully against Hamilton and his followers, calling them a "damned faction" of "British partisans." The newspapers, including the Republican mouthpiece *Aurora*, picked up on his remarks. Now it was Hamilton's turn to be enraged.

Hamilton fired off a letter to Adams asking whether he had truly identified "the existence of a British faction" and "alluded to me" as its leader. When Adams did not reply, Hamilton feverishly penned his "A Letter from Alexander Hamilton Concerning the Public Conduct and Character of John Adams, Esq., President of the United States," and had two hundred copies of the fifty-four-page essay published and distributed among his followers. In it, he blasted Adams for a void of "sound judgment" and surfeit of "a vanity without bounds" and "jealousy capable of discoloring every object." He eviscerated Adams's entire career, condemning virtually every policy or publication he had made along the way. Then, incredibly, Hamilton ended his calumny with the promise that despite all that, he was "resolved not to advise the withholding from him a single vote."[2]

A copy of the essay fell into the hands of Aaron Burr, one of American history's most duplicitous characters.[3] He had copies made and distributed to Republican newspapers across the country. The publication of Hamilton's systematic attack on the character and behavior of Adams was an absolute godsend for the Republicans and completed the Federalist Party's meltdown.

That was not Burr's only machination. He had cut a deal to run as Thomas Jefferson's vice president. But then the votes tied the election with 73 votes each for Jefferson and Burr, 65 for Adams, and 64 for Pinckney. Burr not only refused to release any of his votes to Jefferson but campaigned furiously to swing some of Jefferson's to him. Under the Constitution, the House of Representatives would then vote to break the tie. But after Congress convened on February 11, the deadlock persisted as the representatives remained loyal to the electors of their respective states, and the states remained tied eight to eight. The joint session voted thirty-five times, with each tedious roll call bringing the same result. It was not until the thirty-sixth ballot on February 17, 1801, that a voter switched sides and Jefferson was declared the president.

Ironically, Hamilton put Jefferson over the top. He did so with a "lesser of two evils" appeal to James Bayard, Delaware's sole representative. He lambasted Jefferson for having "politics . . . tinctured with fanaticism" and for having "been a mischievous enemy to the principle measures in our past administration." He condemned him for being "crafty . . . and not scrupulous about the means of success, not very mindful of the truth, and . . . a contemptible hypocrite."[4] Still, he said, Burr was far worse.

Jefferson could have won sooner had he accepted a deal offered by John Adams and Gouverneur Morris. In return for a tie-breaking vote in his favor, he had merely to promise not to explode the national debt, gut the navy, or purge Federalist appointees from the government. But Jefferson spurned the offer. When he entered office, he would be free of any political entanglements with the Federalists.[5]

Adams was bitter not only at his own loss. The Federalist Party had also suffered a crushing defeat. The Republicans captured Congress with 68 to 38 members in the House—almost exactly reversing the 63 to 43 disadvantage in the previous Congress—and a 17 to 15 seat edge in the Senate.[6] Adams was a sore loser; he did not even wait to pass the torch at Jefferson's inaugural but the night before slipped away on the long road to his beloved Quincy.

Nonetheless, John Adams left with his head held high. Like Jefferson, he wanted a message chiseled on his tombstone. Whereas Jefferson deemed three acts of his life worthy of marking his grave, Adams listed only one. In a political career spanning four decades, he wanted to be most remembered as the man "who took upon himself the responsibility of peace with France in the year 1800."[7]

Consequences
Hamiltonism and the Art of American Power

It is the right of every independent nation to pursue its own interests in its own way.
ALEXANDER HAMILTON

What signify a few lives lost in a century or two? The tree of liberty must be refreshed from time to time with the blood of patriots and tyrants. It is its natural manure.
THOMAS JEFFERSON

Perhaps it is a universal truth that the loss of liberty at home is to be charged to the provisions against danger, real or pretended, from abroad.
JAMES MADISON

Some Americans in the early republic understood better than others that wealth is the bottom line of all hard power. Federalists and Republicans held diametrically opposed visions for America's economic future and the relationship among the nation's interests, wealth, and power. Led by Alexander Hamilton's experience, learning, and proposals, the Federalists sought to stimulate a commercial, financial, technological, and industrial revolution. The Republicans feared that such an economic revolution would kill the political revolution. All of that new and concentrated wealth would corrupt the civic virtue that was a republic's foundation. Instead, led by Thomas Jefferson, the Republicans extolled the romantic notion of an agrarian republic of small, autonomous farmers.

A huge battle over America's financial future erupted when, in his 1790 "Report on Public Credit," Hamilton advocated the creation of a Bank of the United States, which would loan money to viable enterprises and the government, regulate a sound national currency, and take over and eliminate the national debt within thirty-four years. Although the bank would be a joint venture of private and public money, the federal government would be its largest shareholder, and the Treasury Department would oversee and regulate its operations. The result would be financial stability and low interest rates, which in turn would give entrepreneurs the capital and confidence with which to invest. This would expand wealth for the nation and revenue for the government. Republicans reacted to Hamilton's plan with horror. They predicted that the bank would lead to concentrations of wealth and political power that would destroy the republic.

The Federalist majority in Congress prevailed, and the Bank of the United States was opened in 1791. But that was only an essential first step in Hamilton's financial revolution. Hamilton was a fiscal conservative who insisted that America abide by the maxim that "the creation of debt should always be accompanied with the means of its extinguishment."[1] An essential role of the bank was to take over and manage America's debt, which included that racked up by the states and by Congress. To that end, Hamilton was eventually able to convince the Republicans to allow the federal government to consolidate all of the public debts into one in return for promising Jefferson and Madison a national capital in the south and a tax rebate for Virginia.

Federalists and Republicans were also at loggerheads over manufacturing. For Federalists, factories were a necessary evil. Machines and mass production increased productivity and thus profits; the larger the scale of production, the larger the profits. The greater the profits, the more money available to reinvest in ways that boosted productivity and profits. And the government could skim some of those profits to invest in ports, roads, schools, and other infrastructure, the skeleton without which the industrial muscle would wither and die. The British had mastered this virtuous economic cycle and were able to mass-produce high-quality, low-priced goods that undersold and often bankrupted local, small-scale producers. In his 1791 "Report on Manufacturing," Hamilton advocated a comprehensive policy that would nurture mass manufacturing and technological innovation in the United States. The choice was stark. The United States could either emulate and surpass the British at mass production or else remain forever dependent on buying their manufactured goods and thus concede wealth and power to America's greatest rival.

The Republicans were content with dependence. They abhorred the very idea of factory labor, which they denounced as being as machinelike as the equipment the workers operated. Even worse, the Republicans hated the vast profits that factory owners amassed. They approved of manufacturing only by craftsmen who, with an apprentice or two, made the entire product. The Republicans won the manufacturing battle by killing Hamilton's proposed industry and technology policy.

A national consensus prevailed on at least one issue. Federalists and Republicans agreed that the United States must act to stop the British and other European powers from curtailing American trade. The Declaration of Independence came with a severe cost beyond the countless shattered lives. The British were sore losers. After signing a peace treaty in 1783, Whitehall restricted what products Americans could sell to Britain and forbade them trade with the West Indies. Americans could only impotently protest. The Articles of Confederation left trade regulation in the hands of the states, which let Britain and the other powers play off each state against the others to the detriment of all.

Ideally that disadvantage should have ended with the 1787 Constitution, which empowered Congress to regulate trade among other duties for managing the economy. But the United States lacked the economic power vital for American diplomats to cut deals that would open British, French, Spanish, and other markets to American goods, and thus aggrandize the nation's wealth and power. The task became ever more difficult after war erupted between Britain and France in 1793. Those countries and their respective allies tried to prevent neutral countries such as the United States from trading with their enemies.

The Americans insisted on their right to trade with all and ally with none. George Washington explained, "It is the sincere wish of United America to have nothing to do with the political intrigues or the squabbles of European nations; but on the contrary, to exchange commodities and live in peace and amity with all the inhabitants of the earth. . . . Under such a system, if we are allowed to pursue it, the agriculture and mechanical arts, the wealth and population of these States will increase with that degree of rapidity as to baffle all calculations." Hamilton put it more succinctly: "It is our true policy to steer as clear as possible of all foreign connections, other than commercial."[2]

That was far easier said than done. Although the two parties shared the goal of trade reciprocity with Britain and other countries, they advocated completely different strategies to achieve it. During the 1780s, some of those who would become Federalists were unabashed economic nationalists who advocated wielding trade like a weapon to assert American interests. As early as 1785, Adams warned Jefferson, "If we cannot obtain reciprocal Liberality, we must adopt reciprocal Prohibitions, Exclusions, Monopolies, and Imposts. We must not be the Dupes. All foreign nations are taking an ungenerous Advantage of our Symplicity and philosophical Liberality. We must not, my Friend, be the Bubbles of our own Liberal Sentiments."[3]

During the 1790s the challenge of actually running a country gave the Federalists a much more sophisticated understanding of the limits of American power. The United States suffered some debilitating economic weaknesses. It had no significant financial or manufacturing industries. It remained dependent on British markets and factory goods for most of its trade. Given the American aversion to taxes, the government had to rely on tariffs for most of its revenues. With those vulnerabilities, the only sensible policy was to be patient and carefully nurture America's economy until it was strong enough to prevail in a trade war. A premature play of the trade card would hurt the United States far more than its target. As John Jay put it, "It is manifestly as much their interest to be well with us as it is ours to be well with them."[4]

Thus the Federalists had a healthy respect for, indeed fear of, British military and economic power. They sought first to develop America's economy and military before they squared off against the British in either sphere, and only then if vital national interests were at stake and all other possible ways to resolve the dispute were exhausted. That meant tolerating British discrimination until America had the economic and military clout to prevail. Yet the United States could take limited steps to even the trade odds over the short run. In the eleventh essay of the Federalist Papers, Hamilton explained, "If we continue united, we may oblige foreign countries to bid against each other for the privileges of our markets."[5]

Those who would become known as Republicans did not experience the same intellectual transformation. They believed that Britain was dependent on the United States and thus could be brought to its knees if America played the trade card. Madison explained that Britain's "dependence as a commercial and manufacturing nation is so absolutely upon us that it gives a moral certainty that her restrictions will not, for her own sake, be prejudicial to our trade." He pointed out that the United States exported "necessities" to Britain in exchange for "superfluities." That gave the United States "natural advantages which no other nation does," and thus "we have abundantly the power to vindicate our cause." The United States could bring Britain to its knees by severing all bilateral trade. Jefferson was gleeful in insisting that Britain's trade "interest . . . is her ruling passion. When they shall see decidedly that . . . we shall suppress their commerce with us, they will be agitated by their avarice on one hand, and their hatred and their fear of us on the other."[6]

Guided by Hamilton, the Washington and Adams presidencies staved off Republican pressure to wage an economic war that would have hurt America much more than it would its adversaries. Yet, at the end, they had little to show for their efforts. Republicans excoriated the Jay Treaty for failing to achieve reciprocity between the United States and Britain. Although Adams did take the nation into the Quasi-War with France over freedom of the seas and trade, he relegated himself and his party to the political wilderness with his administration's excesses, follies, and conceits, culminating with the unconstitutional repressive measures of the Sedition Act. The Federalist Party ultimately self-destructed because it failed to heed perhaps the most vital principle of power: to know its limits.

Yet, if Hamilton's Federalist Party was fleeting, the legacy of his political, economic, and military reforms endured. In a mere dozen years Hamilton led the transformation of the United States from a confederation of sovereign states buried in debt into an economically dynamic, unified nation. And in doing so, he proved to be a true master of the art of American power.

Abbreviations

Adams Papers	John Adams, *The Papers of John Adams*, ed. Robert J. Taylor, Mary-Jo Kline, and Gregg L. Lint, 15 vols. (Cambridge, MA: Harvard University Press, 1977–2010).
Adams Works	John Adams, *The Works of John Adams, Second President of the United States*, ed. Charles Francis Adams, 10 vols. (Boston: Little, Brown, 1850–56).
AECPEU	*Archives Etrangeres, Correspondance Politique, Etats-Unis, Archive National, Paris, France*
AHR	*American Historical Review*
Annals	*Annals of the Congress of the United States*, 42 vols. (Washington, DC: Gales and Seaton, 1834–56).
ASPCN	*American State Papers: Commerce and Navigation*, 2 vols. (Washington, DC: Gales and Seaton, 1832–59).
ASPFR	*American State Papers: Foreign Relations*, 6 vols. (Washington, DC: Gales and Seaton, 1832–59).

ASPMisc   *American State Papers: Miscellaneous*, 2 vols.
                                (Washington, DC: Gales and Seaton, 1832–59).

British Instructions   Bernard Mayo, ed., *The Instructions to the Ministers to the
                                United States, 1791–1812*, vol. 3 of *Annual Report of the
                                American Historical Association, 1936* (Washington, DC:
                                Government Printing Office, 1941).

CFM   Frederick J. Turner, ed., *Correspondence of the French
                                Ministers to the United States, 1791–1797, Annual Report
                                of the American Historical Society of the Year 1903*
                                (Washington, DC: Government Printing Office, 1904).

CPJJ   Henry P. Johnston, ed., *The Correspondence and Public
                                Papers of John Jay* (New York: G. P. Putnam's Sons,
                                1890–93).

Diplomatic Dispatches   Diplomatic Dispatches from France, State Department,
                                National Archives

Hamilton Papers   Alexander Hamilton, *The Papers of Alexander Hamilton*,
                                ed. Harold C. Syrett and Jacob E. Cooke, 27 vols. (New
                                York: Columbia University Press, 1961–87).

Hamilton Works   Alexander Hamilton, *The Works of Alexander Hamilton*,
                                ed. Henry Cabot Lodge, 12 vols. (New York: Putnam,
                                1904).

JAH   *Journal of American History*

Jay Correspondence   John Jay, *The Correspondence and Public Papers of John
                                Jay*, ed. Henry P. Johnston, 4 vols. (New York: Putnam,
                                1890–93).

Jefferson Papers   Thomas Jefferson, *Papers*, ed. Julian P. Boyd et al., 33
                                vols. (Princeton, NJ: Princeton University Press, 1950–
                                2006).

Jefferson Works   Thomas Jefferson, *The Works of Thomas Jefferson*, ed. Paul
                                Leicester Ford, 12 vols. (New York: Putnam, 1904–5).

Jefferson Writings	Thomas Jefferson, *The Writings of Thomas Jefferson*, ed. Andrew A. Lipscomb, 20 vols. (Washington, DC: Thomas Jefferson Memorial Association of the United States, 1905).
LC	Library of Congress
Madison Papers	William T. Huchinson and William M. E. Rachal, eds., *The Papers of James Madison*, 17 vols. (Chicago: University of Chicago Press, 1962–91).
Madison Writings	James Madison, *The Writings of James Madison*, ed. Gaillard Hunt, 9 vols. (New York: Putnam, 1900–10).
Monroe Writings	James Monroe, *The Writings of James Monroe*, ed. Stanislaus Murray Hamilton, 7 vols. (New York: Putnam, 1898–1903).
MVHR	*Mississippi Valley Historical Review*
Presidential Messages	James D. Richardson, *A Compilation of the Messages and Papers of the Presidents*, 10 vols. (Washington, DC: Government Printing Office, 1973).
PRO FO	Public Record Office, (National Archives) Foreign Office, Kew, Britain
Washington Diaries	Donald D. Jackson and Dorothy Twohig, eds., *The Diaries of George Washington*, 6 vols. (Charlottesville: University of Virginia Press, 1976–79).
Washington Writings	George Washington, *The Writings of George Washington from the Original Manuscript Sources, 1745–1799*, ed. John C. Fitzpatrick, 39 vols. (Washington, DC: Government Printing Office, 1931–44).
WMQ	*William and Mary Quarterly*

Notes

Introduction

1. For accounts of the inauguration, see Willard Sterne Randall, *George Washington: A Life* (New York: Henry Holt, 1997), 448–49; David McCullough, *John Adams* (New York: Touchstone, 2001), 402–5.

2. Unless otherwise noted, I have taken details from this brief account of Hamilton's character and career from Ron Chernow, *Alexander Hamilton* (New York: Penguin, 2004); and Willard Sterne Randall, *Alexander Hamilton: A Life* (New York: Harper Perennial, 2003). See also Louis M. Hacker, *Alexander Hamilton in the American Tradition* (New York: McGraw-Hill, 1957); Broadus Mitchell, *Alexander Hamilton: The National Adventure, 1788–1804* (New York: Macmillan, 1962); John C. Miller, *Alexander Hamilton: Portrait in Paradox* (New York: Harper and Row, 1964); Forrest McDonald, *Alexander Hamilton: A Biography* (New York: Norton, 1982); Jacob E. Cooke, *Alexander Hamilton* (New York: Macmillan, 1982).

3. Clinton Rositer, *Alexander Hamilton and the Constitution* (New York: Harcourt, 1964); Gerald Stourzh, *Alexander Hamilton and the Idea of Republican Government* (Stanford, CA: Stanford University Press, 1970).

4. Benjamin Wright, ed., *The Federalist Papers: The Famous Papers on the Principles of American Government* (New York: Barnes and Noble, 1961), 108.

Chapter 1: The Father of His Country

1. Stanley Elkins and Eric McKitrick, *The Age of Federalism: The Early American Republic, 1788–1800* (New York: Oxford University Press, 1993), 34. For two good political biographies of Washington, see Richard Norton Smith, *Patriarch: George Washington and the New American Nation* (New York: Houghton Mifflin, 1993), and Willard Sterne Randall, *George Washington: A Life* (New York: Henry Holt, 1997).

2. Merrill Jensen et al., eds., *The Documentary History of the First Federal Elections, 1788–1790* (Madison: University of Wisconsin Press, 1976–89); Charlene B. Bickford and Kenneth R. Bowling, *The Birth of the Nation: The First Federal Congress, 1789–1791* (Madison: University of Wisconsin Press, 1989).

3. Randall, *Washington*, 449.

4. After Randall, interesting single-volume interpretations of Washington's life include James Thomas Flexner, *Washington: The Indispensable Man* (Boston: Little, Brown, 1969); Forrest McDonald, *The Presidency of George Washington* (Lawrence: University of Kansas Press, 1974); Gary Wills, *Cincinnatus: George Washington and the Enlightenment* (Garden City, NY: Doubleday, 1982).

5. Randall, *Washington*, 96.

6. For an excellent inside account of Washington the executive, see Smith, *Patriarch*.

Chapter 2: Hamilton versus Jefferson

1. For the best analysis, see Ron Chernow, *Alexander Hamilton* (New York: Penguin, 2004). For another excellent analysis, see Willard Sterne Randall, *Alexander Hamilton: A Life* (New York: Harper Perennial, 2003).

2. For two excellent analyses of his character, see Fawn Brodie, *Thomas Jefferson: An Intimate History* (New York: Norton, 1974); Joseph Ellis, *American Sphinx: The Character of Thomas Jefferson* (New York: Alfred Knopf, 1998).

3. Thomas Jefferson, *Notes on the State of Virginia*, ed. William Peden (Chapel Hill: University of North Carolina Press, 1955), 85, 164–65, 174.

4. Ibid., 164.

5. Ibid., 165.

6. Ellis, *American Sphinx*, 673–76.

7. For the best overall analysis, see Irving Brant, *James Madison*, 6 vols. (Indianapolis: Bobbs-Merrill, 1941–61).

8. Stanley Elkins and Eric McKitrick, *The Age of Federalism: The Early American Republic, 1788–1800* (New York: Oxford University Press, 1993), 79.

9. T. V. Smith, "Saints: Secular and Sacerdotal—James Madison and Mahatma Gandhi," *Ethics* 59 (October 1948): 52.

10. For an overview of the differences between the Federalists and Republicans, see Claude G. Bowers, *Jefferson and Hamilton* (Boston: Houghton Mifflin, 1925); Bernard Bailyn, *The Origins of American Politics* (New York: Vintage, 1970); Richard Hofstadter, *The Idea of a Party System: The Rise of Legitimate Opposition in the United States, 1780–1840* (Berkeley: University of California Press, 1970); Richard Buel, *Securing the Revolution: Ideology in American Politics, 1789–1815* (Ithaca, NY: Cornell University Press, 1972); Rudolph Bell, *Party and Faction in American Politics: The House of Representatives, 1789–1801* (Westport, CT: Praeger, 1973); John F. Hoadley, *The Origins of the American Political Parties, 1789–1803* (Lexington: University of

Kentucky Press, 1986); John Zvesper, *Political Philosophy and Rhetoric: A Study of the Origins of American Party Politics* (New York: Cambridge University Press, 1997). For the Federalists, see Leonard White, *The Federalists: A Study in Administrative History* (New York: Macmillan, 1967); Lisle A. Rose, *Prologue to Democracy: The Federalists in the South, 1789–1800* (Lexington: University of Kentucky Press, 1968); Gary Wills, *Explaining America: The Federalists* (Garden City, NY: Doubleday, 1981); Doron S. Ben-Altar and Barbara Oberg, eds., *The Federalists Reconsidered* (Charlottesville: University of Virginia Press, 1998). For the Republicans, see Stuart Gerry Brown, *The First Republicans: The Political Philosophy and Public Policy in the Party of Jefferson and Madison* (Syracuse, NY: Syracuse University Press, 1954); Noble E. Cunningham, *The Jeffersonian Republicans: The Formation of Party Organization, 1789–1801* (Chapel Hill: University of North Carolina Press, 1957); Lance Banning, *The Jeffersonian Persuasion: Evolution of a Party Ideology* (Ithaca, NY: Cornell University Press, 1978).

Chapter 3: Nurturing American Power

1. Catherine Drinker Bowen, *Miracle at Philadelphia: The Story of the Constitutional Convention, May to September 1787* (Boston: Little, Brown, 1966), 122.

2. Robert A. Rutland, *The Birth of the Bill of Rights, 1776–1791* (Chapel Hill: University of North Carolina Press, 1955); Helen Veit, et al., eds., *Creating the Bill of Rights: The Documentary Record from the First Federal Congress* (Baltimore: Johns Hopkins University Press, 1991).

3. Donald F. Swanson, *The Origins of Hamilton's Fiscal Policies* (Gainesville: Florida State University Press, 1963); E. James Ferguson, *The Power of the Purse: A History of American Public Finance, 1776–1790* (Chapel Hill: University of North Carolina Press, 1961); Gilbert L. Lycan, *Alexander Hamilton and American Foreign Policy* (Norman: University of Oklahoma Press, 1970).

4. Benjamin Wright, ed., *The Federalist Papers: The Famous Papers on the Principles of American Government* (New York: Barnes and Noble, 1961), 138, 142.

5. Ferguson, *Power of the Purse*, 330, 332–33.

6. Samuel Flagg Bemis, *Jay's Treaty: A Study in Commerce and Diplomacy* (New York: Macmillan, 1923), 33–35.

7. Ibid., 38.

8. Alexander Hamilton to Thomas Jefferson, January 13, 1791, *Hamilton Works*, 4:348.

9. Wright, *Federalist Papers*, 317–24.

10. Jacob Cooke, "The Compromise of 1790," *WMQ* 27 (October 1970): 523–45; Kenneth R. Bowling, "Dinner at Jefferson's: A Note on Jacob E. Cooke's 'The Compromise of 1790,'" *WMQ* 38 (April 1976): 314; Kenneth R. Bowling, *The Creation of Washington, D.C.: The Idea and Location of the American Capital* (Fairfax, VA: George Mason University Press, 1991), 67–75; Norman Risjord, *Chesapeake Politics, 1781–1800* (New York: Columbia University Press, 1978), 362–93; Forrest McDonald, *Alexander Hamilton: A Biography* (New York: Norton, 1982), 181–88; Stanley Elkins and Eric McKitrick, *The Age of Federalism: The Early American Republic, 1788–1800* (New York: Oxford University Press, 1993), 146–61.

11. Thomas Jefferson to George Washington, September 9, 1792, *Jefferson Papers*, 24:352.

12. Edward Cooke, *The Reports of Alexander Hamilton* (New York: Macmillan, 1982).

13. Bemis, *Jay's Treaty*, 40. For overviews of America's economic development, see Joseph Dorfman, *The Economic Mind in American Civilization, 1606–1865* (New York: Harper, 1964); Curtis P. Nettels, *The Emergence of a National Economy, 1775–1815* (New York: Holt, Rinehart, and Winston, 1962); Stuart Bruchey, *Enterprise: The Dynamic Economy of a Free People* (Cambridge, MA: Harvard University Press, 1990). For trade, see Vernon G. Setser, *The Commercial Reciprocity Policy of the United States, 1774–1829* (Philadelphia: University of Pennsylvania Press, 1937). For finance, see Paul Studenski and Herman E. Kroos, *The Financial History of the United States* (New York: Beard Books, 1963); Ferguson, *Power of the Purse*; Bray Hammond, *Banks and Politics in America, from the Revolution to the Civil War* (Princeton, NJ: Princeton University Press, 1957).

14. For an overview, see Richard H. Kohn, *Eagle and Sword: The Federalists and the Creation of the Military Establishment in America, 1783–1802* (New York: Free Press, 1975); Reginald Stuart, *War and American Thought: From the Revolution to the Monroe Doctrine* (Kent, OH: Kent State University Press, 1982). For the army, see James R. Jacobs, *The Beginnings of the U.S. Army, 1783–1812* (Princeton, NJ: Princeton University Press, 1947); John K. Mahon, *The American Militia: Decade of Decision, 1789–1800* (Gainesville: University of Florida Press, 1960); Paul Prucha, *The Sword of the Republic: The United States Army on the Frontier, 1783–1846* (Lincoln: University of Nebraska Press, 1969); Lawrence Cress, *Citizens in Arms: The Army and the Militia in American Society to the War of 1812* (Chapel Hill: University of North Carolina Press, 1982). For the navy, see Marshall Smelser, *The Congress Founds a Navy, 1787–1798* (Notre Dame, IN: Notre Dame University Press, 1959); Harold and Margaret Sprout, *The Rise of American Naval Power, 1776–1918* (Princeton, NJ: Princeton University Press, 1966).

Chapter 4: Frontier War

1. For three excellent overviews, see Howard Peckham, *The Colonial Wars, 1689–1762* (Chicago: University of Chicago Press, 1964); Douglas Edward Leach, *The Roots of Conflict: British Armed Forces and Colonial Americans, 1677–1763* (Chapel Hill: University of North Carolina Press, 1986); and Ian Steele, *Warpaths: Invasions of North America* (New York: Oxford University Press, 1994).

2. Unless otherwise noted, this section's information comes from Wiley Sword, *President Washington's Indian War: The Struggle for the Old Northwest, 1790–1795* (Norman: University of Oklahoma Press, 1993).

3. "Opinion of General Officers," March 9, 1792, *Washington Writings*, 31:509–15.

4. Andrew J. Birtle, "The Origin of the Legion of the United States," *Journal of Military History* 67 (October 2003): 1249–62.

Chapter 5: British Intrigues

1. Grenville to Dorchester, October 21, 1789, C.A.Q., 42, 153, in *Jay's Treaty: A Study in Commerce and Diplomacy*, by Samuel Flagg Bemis (New York: Macmillan, 1923), 44; Samuel Bemis, "Relations between the Vermont Separatists and Great Britain, 1789–1791," *AHR* 21 (April 1916): 547–60; Frank T. Reuter, "'Petty Spy' or Effective Diplomat: The Role of George Beckwith," *Journal of the Early Republic* 10, no. 4 (Winter 1990), 471–92.

2. Bemis, *Jay's Treaty*, 65–66.

3. Julian Boyd, *Number 7: Alexander Hamilton's Secret Attempts to Control American Foreign Policy* (Princeton, NJ: Princeton University Press, 1964).

4. Hamilton's conversation with Beckwith, October 1790, *Hamilton Papers*, 5:479, 483–84.

5. Thomas Jefferson to Gouverneur Morris, August 12, 1790, *Jefferson Writings*, 5:225. See also George Washington to Gouverneur Morris, October 13, 1789, *Washington Writings*, 30:440–42.

6. Leeds to Gouverneur Morris, April 28, 1790; Gouverneur Morris to George Washington, May 1, 1790, *Washington Writings*, 30:495, 499; Gouverneur Morris to George Washington, May 29, 1790, *ASPFR*, 1:123–25.

7. Gouverneur Morris, *A Diary of the French Revolution, by Gouverneur Morris, 1752–1816, Minister to France during the Terror*, ed. Beatrix Cary Davenport (Westport, CT: Greenwood Publishing, 1972), 1:520–23; Morris to Washington, May 29, 1790, *ASPFR*, 1:123–25.

8. Gouverneur Morris to George Washington, May 29, 1790, *ASPFR*, 1:123–25. See also Gouverneur Morris to George Washington, May 1, 1790, *Washington Papers*, 16:532–35.

9. Gouverneur Morris to George Washington, September 18, November 22, 1790, in Morris, *Diary of the French Revolution*, 1:604, 613.

10. Grenville to Dorchester, June 5, 1790, C.A.Q., 441, 161; Dorchester to George Beckwith, June 27, 1790, in Boyd, *Number 7*, 143–44.

11. Hamilton to George Washington, memorandum, July 8, 15, 1790, *Hamilton Papers*, 6:484–86, 495; *Washington Diaries*, July 8, 1790, 4:137–38. For a good summary of the policy that emerged, see George Washington to Lafayette, August 11, 1790, *Washington Writings*, 31:85–88.

12. "Heads of Proposals on the Nootka Crisis," July 12, 1790, *Jefferson Writings*, 5:200.

13. Hamilton policy proposals, July 12, September 15, 1790, *Hamilton Works*, 4:329, 333–42.

14. "Heads of Proposals on the Nootka Crisis," 200. See also "Outline of Policy on the Mississippi Question," August 2, 1790, *Jefferson Papers*, 17:113–16, 129–30.

15. Thomas Jefferson to Gouverneur Morris, August 12, 1790; Thomas Jefferson to David Humphreys, August 11, 1790; Thomas Jefferson to William Carmichael, August 12, 1790; Thomas Jefferson to William Short, August 10, 26, 1790, *Jefferson Writings*, 5: 122–23, 121, 123–24, 124, 294.

16. Beckwith Report, enclosed in Dorchester to Grenville, September 25, 1790, PRO FO 42, 69. See also George Beckwith to Grenville, November 3, 1790, PRO FO 4, 12.

17. Beckles Willson, *Friendly Relations: A Narrative of Britain's Ministers and Ambassadors to America, 1791–1930* (Freeport, NY: Books for Libraries Press, 1969).

18. "Hawkesbury's Draft of Instructions to Hammond," "Grenville Instructions to Hammond," in *Instructions to the British Ministers to the United States, 1791–1812*, by Bernard Mayo (New York: Da Capo Press, 1971).

19. Jefferson to Hammond, November 29, December 5, 13, 15, 1791; Hammond to Jefferson, November 30, December 6, 14, 19, 1791, *Jefferson Papers*, 22:352–53, 356–57, 378–79, 380–81, 399, 402–3, 409–11, 422.

20. Hammond to Grenville, December 19 (Dispatch 13), January 9 (Dispatch 3), PRO FO 4/11, III, PRO FO 4/14, II; "Conversation with George Beckwith," May 15, 1791, *Hamilton Papers*, 8:432–43.

21. Hamilton to Jefferson, May 20–27, 1792, *Hamilton Papers*, 11:408–11; Jefferson to Hammond, May 29, 1792, *Jefferson Papers*, 23:196–212; Jefferson to Madison, June 4, 1792, *Jefferson Writings*, 7:100–102.

Chapter 6: Spanish Stonewalling

1. Carondelet Military Report, November 24, 1794, in *Louisiana under the Rule of Spain, France, and the United States*, ed. James A. Robertson, 2 vols. (Cleveland: A. H. Clark, 1911), 1:298.

2. Thomas Jefferson to George Washington, March 24, 1790, *Washington Diaries*, 4:108.

3. Thomas Jefferson to William Short, August 26, 1790, *Jefferson Papers*, 5:218. See also "Outline of Policy on the Mississippi Question," August 2, 1790, *Jefferson Papers*, 17:129–30; Thomas Jefferson to William Carmichael, August 12, 1790, *Jefferson Writings*, 5:224; Thomas Jefferson to Harry Innes, March 13, 1790, *Jefferson Papers*, 5:294.

4. Samuel Flagg Bemis, *Pinckney's Treaty: A Study in America's Advantage from Europe's Distress, 1783–1800* (Baltimore: Johns Hopkins Press, 1926), 327, 330, 332.

5. John Walton Caughey, *McGillivray of the Creeks* (Columbia: University of South Carolina Press, 2007).

6. Thomas Jefferson to George Washington, April 2, 1791, *Jefferson Writings*, 6:239.

Chapter 7: America and the French Revolution

1. G. Adolf Koch, *Republican Religion: The American Revolution and the Cult of Reason* (New York: P. Smith, 1964); Bernard Faÿ, *The Revolutionary Spirit in France and America: A Study of Moral and Intellectual Relations between France and the United States at the End of the Eighteenth Century* (New York: Harcourt, Brace, 1955).

2. Jefferson to William Short, January 3, 1793, *Jefferson Writings*, 6:153–56.

3. Melanie Randolph Miller, ed., *The Diaries of Gouverneur Morris: European Travels, 1794–1798* (Charlottesville: University of Virginia Press, 2011).

4. Thomas Jefferson to William Short, October 16, 1792, *Jefferson Writings*, 6:122; George Washington to Gouverneur Morris, January 28, 1792, *Washington Writings*, 31:468–70.

5. William Short to Gouverneur Morris, September 7, 1792, *ASPFR*, 1:341; George Washington to Thomas Jefferson, March 13, 1793, *Washington Writings*, 32:385–86; Thomas Jefferson to Gouverneur Morris, March 15, 1793, *Jefferson Writings*, 6:202–3.

Chapter 8: The Widening National Rift

1. Alexander DeConde, *Entangling Alliance: Politics and Diplomacy under George Washington* (Durham, NC: Duke University Press, 1958), 141–63.

2. Lewis Leary, *That Rascal Freneau: A Study in Literary Failure* (New Brunswick, NJ: Rutgers University Press, 1941).

3. Kenneth Martis, *The Historical Atlas of Political Parties in the United States Congress* (New York: Macmillan, 1989).

4. Jefferson to Adams, May 13, 1791; Adams to Jefferson, July 29, 1791, The Thomas Jefferson Papers Series, American Memory from the Library of Congress, http://hd1.loc.gov/loc.mss.

5. "American," August 4, 1792, *Gazette of the United States*; Washington to Hamilton, July 29, 1792; Hamilton to Washington, August 3, 1792, *Hamilton Papers*, 12:129–34, 139.

6. See William T. Hutchinson and William M. E. Rachal, eds. *The Papers of James Madison*, 17 vols., (Chicago: University of Chicago Press, 1962–91), 14:117–22, 137–39, 170, 178–79, 191–92, 197–98, 201–2, 206–8, 217–18, 233–34, 244–46, 257–59, 266–68, 274–75, 370–72, 426–27; I:302–9; 17:559–60.

7. Alexander Hamilton to William Short, February 5, 1793, *Hamilton Works*, 8:292.

8. George Washington to Thomas Jefferson, August 23, 1792; George Washington to Alexander Hamilton, August 26, 1792, *Washington Writings*, 32:128–34.

Chapter 9: The Second Term Team

1. Kenneth C. Martis, *The Historical Atlas of Political Parties in the United States Congress* (New York: Macmillan, 1989).

2. Thomas Jefferson to George Washington, September 9, 1792, *Jefferson Writings*, 6:109.

Chapter 10: The Genêt Wild Card

1. Howard Mumford Jones, *America and French Culture, 1750–1848* (Chapel Hill: University of North Carolina Press, 1927); Elizabeth B. White, *American Opinion of France, from Lafayette to Poincare* (New York: Alfred A. Knopf, 1927); Louis Martin Sears, *George Washington and the French Revolution* (Westport, CT: Greenwood Press, 1975).

2. Meade Minnegerode, *Jefferson, Friend of France, 1793: The Career of Edmond Charles Genêt* (New York: Putnam, 1929); Harry Ammon, "The Genêt Mission and the Development of American Political Parties," *Journal of American History* 52 (March 1966): 725–41; Harry Ammon, *The Genêt Mission* (New York: Norton, 1971).

3. Washington to Heads of Departments, "Questions Submitted to the Cabinet," April 18, 1793, *Washington Writings*, 32:415–16, 419–21; "Cabinet Opinion on Proclamation and French Minister," April 19, 1793, Jefferson to Washington, April 28, 1793, "Opinion on French Treaties," April 28, 1793, *Jefferson Writings*, 6:217–31; Hamilton and Knox to Washington, May 2, 1793, Hamilton to Washington, May 2, 1793, *Hamilton Papers*, 14:367–96, 398–408.

4. Charles C. Hyneman, *The First American Neutrality: A Study of the American Understanding of Neutral Obligations during the Years 1792 to 1815* (Urbana: University of Illinois Press, 1934); Alexander DeConde, *Entangling Alliance: Politics and Diplomacy under George Washington* (Durham: Duke University Press, 1958); Albert H. Bowman, *The Struggle for Neutrality: Franco-American Diplomacy during the Federalist Era* (Knoxville: University of Tennessee Press, 1974).

5. Thomas Jefferson to Gouverneur Morris, March 12, 1793, *Jefferson Writings*, 6:199.

6. Washington, Proclamation, April 22, 1793, *Washington Writings*, 32:430–31; Helvidius, *Madison Writings*, 6:186. See Charles Marion Ammon, *American Neutrality in 1793: A Study in Cabinet Government* (New York: AMS Press, 1967).

7. Thomas Jefferson to Jean Baptiste de Ternant, May 3, 15, 1793, *Jefferson Writings*, 6:236–37, 254–57.

8. Genêt to Foreign Affairs Minister, August 15, 1793, CFM, 241.

9. Jefferson to Gênet, June 1, 17, 19, 1793, Genêt to Jefferson, June 8, 14, 1793, ASPFR 1:151, 156–58; Jefferson to Washington, June 6, 1793, *Jefferson Writings*, 6:287–89; "Anas," July 5, August 23, 1793, *Jefferson Writings*, 1:235–37, 262; Genêt to Foreign Minister, August 15, October 5, 1793, CFM, 241, 258; Samuel F. Bemis, "Payment of the French Loans to the United States, 1777–1795," *Current History* 23 (March 1926): 824–36.

10. Genêt to Jefferson, June 22, 1793, ASPFR, 1:158–59.

11. "Anas," July 5, 1793, *Jefferson Writings*, 1:235–37.

12. Frederick J. Turner, "Documents on the Relations of France to Louisiana, 1792–95," *AHR* 3 (April 1898): 499–516; Frederick J. Turner, "The Origins of Genet's Projected Attack on Louisiana and the Floridas," *AHR* 3 (July 1898): 650–71; Frederick J. Turner, "The Policy of France toward the Mississippi Valley in the Period of Washington and Adams," *AHR* 10 (January 1905): 249–79.

13. Genêt to Michaux, July 12, 1793, Genêt Papers, LC, 10:307; Thomas Jefferson to Isaac Shelby, August 29, 1793, ASPFR, 1:455; "Journal of André Michaux, 1793–1796," in *Early Western Travels, 1748–1846*, ed. Reuben G. Thwaites, 32 vols. (Cleveland: Arthur H. Clarke, 1904–7), 3:27–53; Henry Knox to Arthur St. Clair, November 9, 1793, ASPFR, 1:458; Henry Knox to Anthony Wayne, March 31, 1794, ASPFR, 1:458; Archibald Henderson, "Isaac Shelby and the Genêt Mission," *MVHR* 6 (March 1920): 445–69; F. R. Hall, "Genet's Western Intrigue, 1793–1794," *Illinois State Historical Society Journal* 21 (1928): 359–81; Mildred S. Fletcher, "Louisiana as a Factor in French Diplomacy from 1763–1800," *MVHR* 27 (December 1930): 367–76.

14. Thomas Jefferson to James Madison, July 7, 1793, *Jefferson Writings*, 1:237–41.

15. DeConde, *Entangling Alliance*, 481.

16. "Reasons for the Opinion of the Treasury Secretary and War Secretary Respecting the Brigantine Little Sarah," July 8, 1793, *Hamilton Papers*, 15:75; "Anas," July 10, 1793, *Jefferson Writings*, 1:237–41.

17. George Washington to Thomas Jefferson, July 11, 1793, *Washington Writings*, 33:4.

18. Thomas Jefferson to Edmond Genêt, July 12, 1793, ASPFR, 1:163.

19. Thomas Jefferson to the Supreme Court, July 18, 1793, Thomas Jefferson to James Madison, August 3, 1793, *Jefferson Writings*, 6:258–59, 351–52; John Jay and Supreme Court to George Washington, August 8, 1793, *Jay Correspondence*, 3:488–89.

20. "Instructions to the Collectors of the Customs," August 4, 1793, *Hamilton Works*, 4:236–41; George Washington to Department Heads, July 29, 1793, George Washington to Thomas Jefferson, August 4, 1793, *Washington Writings*, 33:34, 37–38.

21. Thomas Jefferson to Gouverneur Morris, August 16, 1793, Memorandum to France, August 16, 1793, *ASPFR* 1:167–74.

22. Eugene P. Link, *Democratic-Republican Societies, 1790–1800* (New York: Columbia University Press, 1942); Philip S. Foner, ed., *The Democratic Republican Societies, 1790–1800: A Documentary Sourcebook* (Westport, CT: Greenwood Press, 1976); John R. Howe, "Republican Thought and the Political Violence of the 1790s," *American Quarterly* 19 (Summer 1967): 148–65.

23. Donald H. Stewart, *The Opposition Press of the Federalist Period* (Albany: State University Press of New York, 1969).

24. "Pacificus II," Seven Pacific essays, *Hamilton Works*, 4:159, 135–91.

25. Five Helvidius letters, *Madison Writings*, 4:138–88.

26. Thomas Jefferson to James Madison, August 3, 1793, *Jefferson Writings*, 6:361–62; "Anas," August 6, 1793, *Jefferson Writings*, 1:256–59; Thomas Jefferson to George Washington, August 11, 1793, *Jefferson Writings*, 6:366–67.

27. Thomas Jefferson to James Madison, August 11, 1793, *Madison Papers*, 15:56–57.

28. Circular, September 7, 1793, *Jefferson Writings*, 6:417.

29. Thomas Jefferson to Edmond Genêt, September 15, 1793, *Jefferson Writings*, 6:429–30; Edmond Genêt to Thomas Jefferson, September 18, 1793, *ASPFR*, 1:172–74.

30. Gouverneur Morris to Thomas Jefferson, October 10, 1793, Diplomatic Dispatches.

31. Fifth Annual Address to Congress, December 3, 1793, *Washington Writings*, 33:165–69.

32. Neutrality Proclamation, March 24, 1794, *Washington Writings*, 3:304–05.

33. For the most extensive of Fauchet's interesting and perceptive analyses of American politics and Franco-American relations, see Fauchet to foreign minister.

34. Gouverneur Morris to Thomas Jefferson, February 13, 1793, *ASPFR*, 1:350.

35. George Washington to Gouverneur Morris, June 25, 1794, *Washington Writings*, 33:413–14.

Chapter 11: British Aggression and Trade War

1. Grenville to Hammond, March 12, 1793, no. 6, PRO FO 115/2.

2. Samuel Flagg Bemis, *Jay's Treaty: A Study in Commerce and Diplomacy* (New York: Macmillan, 1923), 159.

3. Alexander DeConde, *Entangling Alliance: Politics and Diplomacy under George Washington* (Durham, NC: Duke University Press, 1958), 481.

4. Thomas Jefferson to Thomas Pinckney, June 11, 1792, ASPFR, 3:574; "Report on the Privileges and Restrictions on the Commerce of the United States," *Jefferson Writings*, 6:470–84. For an analysis of the report, see Merrill D. Peterson, "Thomas Jefferson and Commercial Policy, 1783–1793," *WMQ* 22 (October 1965): 584–610.

5. Resolutions, January 3, 1794, *Annals*, 3rd Cong., 1st sess., 155–56.

6. Stanley Elkins and Eric McKitrick, *The Age of Federalism: The Early American Republic, 1788–1800* (New York: Oxford University Press, 1993), 376.

7. Douglass C. North, "The United States Balance of Payments, 1790–1860," in *Trends in the American Economy in the Nineteenth Century*, ed. William Parker (Princeton, NJ: Princeton University Press, 1960), 595; Gordon C. Bjork, "The Weaning of the American Economy: Independence, Market Changes, and Economic Development," *Journal of Economic History* 24 (December 1964): 541–60; Elkins and McKitrick, *Age of Federalism*, 382.

8. *Annals*, 3rd Cong., 1st sess., January 13, 27, 1794), 338–39.

9. Skipwith to Randolph, March 1, 7, 1794, ASPFR, 1:239, 428.

10. Hamilton to Washington, March 8, 1794, *Hamilton Works*, 10:63–65.

11. Madison to Jefferson, March 9 and 12, 1794, *Madison Papers*, 15:274, 279.

12. Dorchester Speech, in *The Correspondence of Lieutenant-Governor John Simcoe*, ed. Ernest A. Cruikshank (Toronto: Ontario Historical Society, 1923–31), 2:149–60.

13. Alexander Hamilton to George Washington, April 14, 1793, *Hamilton Works*, 4:519.

Chapter 12: The Whiskey Rebellion

1. Alexander DeConde, *Entangling Alliance: Politics and Diplomacy under George Washington* (Durham, NC: Duke University Press, 1958), 240.

2. Steven R. Boyd, ed., *The Whiskey Rebellion: Past and Present Perspectives* (Westport, CT: Praeger, 1986); Thomas P. Slaughter, *The Whiskey Rebellion: Frontier Epilogue to the American Revolution* (New York: Oxford University Press, 1986).

3. John K. Mahon, *The American Militia: Decade of Decision, 1789–1800* (Gainesville: University of Florida Press, 1960); Lawrence Cress, *Citizens in Arms: The Army and the Militia in American Society to the War of 1812* (Chapel Hill: University of North Carolina Press, 1982); Don Higginbotham, "The Federalized Militia Debate: A Neglected Aspect of Second Amendment Scholarship," *WMQ*, 3rd. ser., vol. 55, no. 1 (January 1998): 39–58.

4. Hamilton to Washington, August 2, 1794, *Hamilton Papers*, 17:15–19.

5. Mifflin to Washington, August 5, 1794, *ASPMisc*, 1:97–99.

6. Stanley Elkins and Eric McKitrick, *The Age of Federalism: The Early American Republic, 1788–1800* (New York: Oxford University Press, 1993), 483, 484.

Chapter 13: Winning the West

1. Reginald Horsman, "The British Indian Department and the Resistance to General Anthony Wayne, 1793–1795," *MVHR* 49 (September 1962): 269–90; J. Leitch Wright, *Britain and the American Frontier, 1783–1815* (Athens: University of Georgia Press, 1975).

2. Samuel Flagg Bemis, *Jay's Treaty: A Study in Commerce and Diplomacy* (New York: Macmillan, 1923), 163.

3. Isabel Thompson, *Joseph Brant, 1743–1807, A Man of Two Worlds* (Syracuse, NY: Syracuse University Press, 1984).

4. Timothy Pickering to George Washington, March 21, 1792, *Hamilton Papers*, 11:377.

5. Bemis, *Jay's Treaty*, 181.

Chapter 14: The Jay Treaty

1. Samuel Flagg Bemis, *Jay's Treaty: A Study in Commerce and Diplomacy* (New York: Macmillan, 1923); Jerald A. Combs, *The Jay Treaty: Political Battleground of the Founding Fathers* (Berkeley: University of California Press, 1970).

2. Alexander Hamilton to George Washington, "Points to Be Considered in the Instructions to Mr. Jay," April 23, 1794, Alexander Hamilton to John Jay, May 6, 1794, *Hamilton Works*, 16:282–83, 320; Jay's Instructions, May 6, 1794, *ASPFR*, 1:472–74.

3. John Jay to Alexander Hamilton, July 11, 1794, John Jay to Edmund Randolph, June 12, 1794, John Jay to George Washington, September 13, 1784, *Jay Correspondence*, 4:29, 30, 59.

4. Jay to Washington, June 23, 1794, *ASPFR*, 4:26; Jay to Randolph, July 6, 9, 1794, numbers 1 and 4, *ASPFR*, 1:477, 479; Jay to Hamilton, July 11, 1794, *Hamilton Papers*, 16:608–9.

5. David Geggus, "The Cost of Pitt's Caribbean Campaigns, 1793–1798," *The Historical Journal* 26, no. 3 (1983): 699–706.

6. Samuel Bemis argues that it did; Jerald Combs disagrees. Bemis, *Jay's Treaty*, 246–51, 337–45; Combs, *Jay Treaty*, 157–58; George Hammond to Grenville, August 3, 1794, PRO FO 5/5.

7. Grenville to John Jay, August 1, 1794, *ASPFR*, 1:481–82.

8. Grenville to Jay, August 30, 1794, *ASPFR*, 1:487–90.

9. Jay to Grenville, September 1 and 4, 1794, John Jay to Edmund Randolph, September 13, 1794, *ASPFR*, 1:490–92, 500; John Jay to George Washington, September 13, 1794, CPJJ, 58–60; John Jay to Edmund Randolph, September 13, 1794, No. 15, Grenville to Jay, September 5,

1794, No. 15, *ASPFR*, 1:485, 493; Samuel Flagg Bemis, "Jay's Treaty an the Northwest Boundary Gap," *AHR* 27 (April 1922): 465–84.

10. "Treaty," November 19, 1794, *ASPFR*, 1:50–55.

11. Camillus letters, *Hamilton Works*, 4:371–524, 5:3–332.

12. Edmund Randolph to George Washington, July 12, 1795, in Worthington C. Ford, ed., "Edmund Randolph on the British Treaty, 1795," *AHR* 12, no. 3 (April 1907): 587–99; George Washington to Edmund Randolph, July 22, 1795, *Washington Writings*, 34:244.

13. Grenville to Hammond, May 9, 1795, no 8, June 4, 1795, no. 12, PRO FO 5/9.

14. Timothy Pickering to George Washington, July 31, 1795, *Washington Writings*, 34:265.

15. Stanley Elkins and Eric McKitrick, *The Age of Federalism: The Early American Republic, 1788–1800* (New York: Oxford University Press, 1993), 425.

16. Ibid., 425–31; Irving Brant, "Edmund Randolph, Not Guilty!" *WMQ* 7 (April 1950): 179–98; W. Allen Wilber, "Oliver Wolcott, Jr., and Edmund Randolph's Resignation, 1795: An Explanatory Note on an Historic Misconception," *Connecticut Historical Society Bulletin* 38 (January 1973): 12–16; Mary K. Bonstee Tachau, "George Washington and the Reputation of Edmund Randolph," *JAH* 73 (June 1986): 15–34.

17. Fauchet to foreign minister, May 7, 1794, CFM, 376.

18. Alexander Hamilton to Oliver Wolcott, August 10, 1795, *Hamilton Works*, 10:113.

19. Alexander Hamilton to Rufus King, April 13, 1796, *Hamilton Works*, 10:159.

20. Minutes of the Cabinet Meeting, January 14, 1796, Grenville to Phineas Bond, January 1796, PRO FO 5/16; Phineas Bond to Grenville, March 31, 1796, no. 17, April 17, 1796, no. 25, PRO FO 5/13.

21. *Annals*, 5:1239–1263; John Adams to Abigail Adams, April 30, 1796, in *Familiar Letters of John Adams to and His Wife Abigail Adams, During the Revolution: With a Memoir of Mrs. Adams* (New York: Nabu Press, 2010), 2:226–27.

22. Charles R. Ritcheson, *Aftermath of Revolution: British Policy toward the United States, 1783–1795* (Dallas: Southern Methodist University Press, 1969), 238–41.

23. Timothy Pickering to Rufus King, June 8, 1796, Rufus King to Grenville, January 28, 1797, *ASPFR*, 2:147–48, 3:574–75.

24. Grenville to Rufus King, March 27, 1797, *ASPFR*, 2:148–50.

Chapter 15: The Pinckney Treaty

1. Samuel Flagg Bemis, *Pinckney's Treaty: A Study in America's Advantage from Europe's Distress, 1783–1800* (Baltimore: Johns Hopkins Press, 1926), 257.

2. Ibid.; Arthur Whitaker, *The Mississippi Question, 1795–1803: A Study in Trade, Politics, and Diplomacy* (New York: C. Appleton Century, 1934); Arthur Whitaker, *The Spanish–American Frontier, 1783–1795: The Westward Movement and the Spanish Retreat in the Mississippi Valley* (Lincoln: University of Nebraska Press, 1969).

3. Bemis, *Pinckney's Treaty*, 264–65.

4. William Short to Thomas Jefferson, November 13, 1793, *Jefferson Papers*, 27:350–51.

5. Bemis, *Pinckney's Treaty*, 212–14.

6. Historians debate whether Godoy knew of the Jay Treaty's content before signing the treaty with Pinckney, with Whitaker arguing that he did and Bemis that he did not. The treaty's text was published in Philadelphia on July 1, 1795, and Monroe had a copy in Paris on August 15, 1795, but no copy of the treaty accompanied dispatches from Jáudenes to Godoy. Whitaker, *Spanish–American Frontier*, 206; Bemis, *Pinckney's Treaty*, 284–93.

7. Bemis, *Pinckney's Treaty*, 275.

Chapter 16: Fraying Ties with France

1. James Monroe to Timothy Pickering, September 15, 1794, *ASPFR*, 1:675.

2. Delacroix to Directory, January 16, 1796, AECPEU, 45:41–53.

3. Timothy Pickering to James Monroe, September 12, 1795, *ASPFR*, 1:596–98; James Monroe to Timothy Pickering, November 5, December 6, 1795, *Monroe Writings*, 2:410, 422–27; Foreign Affairs Minister to James Monroe, March 11, 1796, *ASPFR*, 1:732–33; James Monroe to Foreign Affairs Minister, March 15, 20, 1796, James Monroe to Timothy Pickering, May 2, 1796, *Monroe Writings*, 2: 467–82, 489–92.

4. James Monroe to Thomas Jefferson, June 23, 1795, *Monroe Writings*, 2:292–304.

5. James McHenry to Arthur St. Clair, May 1796, *The St. Clair Papers: The Life and Public Service of Arthur St. Clair*, ed. William Henry Smith, 2 vols. (Cincinnati: Robert Clarke, 1882), 2:395–96; George W. Kyte, "A Spy on the Western Waters: The Military Intelligence Mission of General Collot in 1796," *MVHR* 34 (December 1947): 427–42.

6. Timothy Pickering, Oliver Wolcott, and James McHenry to George Washington, July 2, 1796, *Washington Writings*, 13:216; George Washington to Timothy Pickering, August 10, 1796, George Washington to Oliver Wolcott, August 10, 1796, George Washington to John Marshall, August 10, 1796, *Washington Writings*, 35:174–75, 176–77.

7. Charles Pinckney to Timothy Pickering, November 17, December 10, 20, 26, 1796, February 18, 1797, *ASPFR*, 2:5–10; Foreign Minister to James Monroe, December 11, 1796, *ASPFR* 1:746–47.

Chapter 17: The Farewell Address

1. Washington's Farewell Address, September 19, 1796, *Washington Writings*, 25:214–38; Burton J. Kaufman, ed., *Washington's Farewell Address: The View from the 20th Century* (Chicago:

Quadrangle Books, 1969); Arthur A. Markowitz, "Washington's Farewell and the Historians: A Critical Review," *Pennsylvania Magazine of History and Biography* 94 (April 1970): 173–91.

Chapter 18: John Adams and American Power

1. David McCullough, *John Adams* (New York: Touchstone, 2001); John Ferling, *John Adams: A Life* (New York: Henry Holt, 1992); Page Smith, *John Adams*, 2 vols. (Westport, CT: Greenwood Publishing, 1969).

2. Peter Shaw, *The Character of John Adams* (Chapel Hill: University of North Carolina Press, 1976).

3. *Adams Papers*, 1:7–8.

4. Anas, *Jefferson Writings*, 1:273.

5. Quoted in Alexander DeConde, *The Quasi-War: The Politics and Diplomacy of the Undeclared War with France, 1797–1801* (New York: Scribner, 1966), 4.

6. Jonathan Sewall to Judge Lee, September 2, 1787, quoted in *The Peacemakers: The Great Powers and American Independence*, by Richard Morris (New York: Harper & Row, 1965), 451.

7. Adams to Abigail, December 7, 1796, *Adams Letters to Wife*; Stanley Elkins and Eric McKitrick, *The Age of Federalism: The Early American Republic, 1788–1800* (New York: Oxford University Press, 1993), 533.

8. Correa M. Walsh, *The Political Science of John Adams: A Study in the Theory of Mixed Government and the Bicameral System* (New York: Putnam, 1915); Russell Kirk, *The Conservative Mind, from Burke to Santayana* (Chicago: Chicago University Press, 1955); Peter Viereck, *Conservatism, from John Adams to Churchill* (Princeton, NJ: Princeton University Press, 1956); Edward Handler, *America and Europe in the Political Thought of John Adams* (Cambridge, MA: Harvard University Press, 1964); John R. Howe, *The Changing Political Thought of John Adams* (Princeton, NJ: Princeton University Press, 1966).

9. John Adams to Uriah Forrest, May 13, 1799, *Adams Works*, 8:645–46.

10. Kenneth C. Martis, *The Historical Atlas of Political Parties in the United States Congress* (New York: Macmillan, 1989).

11. Thomas Jefferson, Notes, March 12 to October 13, 1797, inserted May 10, 1797, Jefferson Papers, LC online.

Chapter 19: The XYZ Affair

1. James Brown Scott, ed., *The Controversy over Neutral Rights between the United States and France, 1797–1800: A Collection of American State Papers and Judicial Decisions* (New York: Oxford University Press, 1917); Albert H. Bowman, *The Struggle for Neutrality: Franco-American Diplomacy during the Federalist Era* (Knoxville: University of Tennessee Press, 1974); William Stinchcombe, *The XYZ Affair* (Westport, CT: Praeger, 1980).

2. Stanley Elkins and Eric McKitrick, *The Age of Federalism: The Early American Republic, 1788–1800* (New York: Oxford University Press, 1993), 538.

3. Wattenberg, Statistical History, 750, 907, ASP, Class IV, Commerce and Navigation, 1:362–84, *ASPFR*, 2:30–31, 169–82; Pickering Report to Congress, February 28, 1797, *ASPFR*, 1:748–80l; Michael Palmer, *Stoddert's War: Naval Operations during the Quasi-War with France, 1798–1801* (Columbia: University of South Carolina Press, 1987), 6; Stinchcombe, *XYZ Affair*, 84; Alexander DeConde, *The Quasi-War: The Politics and Diplomacy of the Undeclared War with France, 1797–1801* (New York: Scribner, 1966), 124–26; Bowman, *Struggle for Neutrality*, 108–17, 185–86.

4. Washington to McHenry, April 3, 1797, *Washington Writings*, 35:430.

5. Hamilton to Pickering, March 22, 1797, *Hamilton Papers*, 10:454–55.

6. Adams to Abigail Adams, April 24, 1797, *Adams Letters to Wife*, 2:254.

7. *Presidential Messages*, 1:2–29.

8. John Edward Smith, *John Marshall: Definer of a Nation* (New York: Henry Holt, 1998); Charles Hobson, *The Great Chief Justice: John Marshall and the Rule of Law* (Lawrence: University of Kansas Press, 2000).

9. George A. Billias, *Elbridge Gerry: Founding Father and Republican Statesman* (New York: McGraw Hill, 1976).

10. Marvin B. Zahniser, *Charles Cotesworth Pinckney: Founding Father* (Chapel Hill: University of North Carolina Press, 1967).

11. Charles Pinckney to Timothy Pickering, September 14, 1797, Diplomatic Dispatches, 5 Record Group 59.

12. Stinchcombe, *XYZ Affair*, 55–57; American Envoys to Timothy Pickering, October 22, 1797, Diplomatic Dispatches, 6:59.

13. American Envoys to Pickering, October 22, 1797, *ASPFR*, 2:159.

14. American Envoys to Timothy Pickering, November 8, 1797, Diplomatic Dispatches, 6:59.

15. There are slightly different versions in American Envoys to Pickering, October 27, 1797, *ASPFR*, 2:161; Beveridge, *John Marshall*, 2:271–73.

16. Beveridge, *John Marshall*, 2:291–92; Pinckney note, December 21, 1797, *ASPFR*, 2:167.

17. American Envoys to Timothy Pickering, December 24, 1797, Diplomatic Dispatches, 6:59.

18. Stinchcombe, *XYZ Affair*, 66.

19. American Envoys to Timothy Pickering, March 9, 1798, Diplomatic Dispatches, 6:59.

20. Stinchcombe, *XYZ Affair*, 63–69, 106–7.

21. Ibid., 81, 77–110.

22. DeConde, *Quasi-War*, 58.

Chapter 20: Mustering for War

1. Adams to department heads, March 13 1798, *Adams Papers*, 8:568.

2. William Stinchcombe, *The XYZ Affair* (Westport, CT: Praeger, 1980), 32–33.

3. Richard H. Kohn, *Eagle and Sword: The Federalists and the Creation of the Military Establishment in America, 1783–1802* (New York: Free Press, 1975); Marshall Smelser, *Congress Founds the Navy, 1787–1798* (Notre Dame, IN: Notre Dame University Press, 1959); Craig Symonds, *Navalists and Antinavalists: The Naval Policy Debate in the United States, 1789–1827* (Newark: University of Delaware Press, 1980).

4. Michael Palmer, *Stoddert's War: Naval Operations during the Quasi-War with France, 1798–1801* (Columbia: University of South Carolina Press, 1987), 21, 53.

5. Ibid., 34.

6. *Presidential Messages*, 1:256.

7. David Dewey, *Financial History of the United States* (New York: Adamant Media, 2001), 110–13.

8. Alexander DeConde, *The Quasi-War: The Politics and Diplomacy of the Undeclared War with France, 1797–1801* (New York: Scribner, 1966), 102.

Chapter 21: The War at Home

1. Alexander Hamilton to James McHenry, July 30, 1798, James McHenry to Alexander Hamilton, September 10, 1798, *Hamilton Works*, 6:90–92, 356.

2. John Adams to James McHenry, August 14, 29, 1798, *Adams Works*, 8:587–88, 593–94; James McHenry to John Adams, August 22, 1798, Bernard C. Steiner, *The Life and Correspondence of James McHenry, Secretary of War Under Washington and Adams* (New York: Kessinger Publishing, 2007), 325, 338.

3. Oliver Wolcott to John Adams, September 17, 1798, *Memoirs of the Administrations of Washington and John Adams, Edited from the Papers of Oliver Wolcott, Secretary of the Treasury*, ed. George Gibbs (New York: W. Van Norden, 1846), 2:93–99; George Washington to John Adams, September 25, 1798, *Washington Writings*, 36:453–62; John Adams to George Washington, October 9, 1798, *Adams Works*, 6:600–601; John Adams to James McHenry, October 22, 1798, *Adams Works*, 8:612–13.

4. John C. Miller, *Crisis in Freedom: The Alien and Sedition Acts* (Boston: Little, Brown, 1951); James M. Smith, *Freedom's Fetters: The Alien and Sedition Laws and American Civil Liberties* (Ithaca, NY: Cornell University Press, 1956); Leonard W. Levy, *The Legacy of Suppression: Freedom of Speech and Press in Early American History* (Cambridge, MA: Harvard University Press, 1960).

5. Alexander DeConde, *The Quasi-War: The Politics and Diplomacy of the Undeclared War with France, 1797–1801* (New York: Scribner, 1966), 99.

6. William Watkins, *Reclaiming the American Revolution: The Kentucky and Virginia Resolves and Their Legacy* (New York: Palgrave Macmillan, 2004); Adrienne Koch and Henry Ammon, *Jefferson and Madison: The Great Collaboration* (Old Saybrook, CT: Konecky and Konecky, 2010), 22:552–53.

7. Alexander Hamilton to James McHenry, May 29, 1799, *Hamilton Papers*, 22: 552–53.

Chapter 22: The Quasi-Alliance

1. Grenville to Liston, January 15, 1798, *British Instructions*, 148–49; Bradford Perkins, *The First Rapprochement: England and the United States, 1795–1805* (Berkeley: University of California Press, 1967).

2. Grenville to Liston, January 27, 1797, *British Instructions*, 128–30.

3. William H. Masterson, *William Blount* (Baton Rouge: Louisiana State University Press, 1954); Arthur Whitaker, *The Mississippi Question, 1795–1803: A Study in Trade, Politics, and Diplomacy* (New York: C. Appleton Century, 1934), 104–14; Perkins, *First Rapprochement*, 99–100; Frederick Jackson Turner, ed., "Documents on the Blount Conspiracy, 1795–1797," AHR 10, no. 3 (April 1905): 582–83.

4. William Pitt to Francisco de Miranda, quoted in Alexander DeConde, *The Quasi-War: The Politics and Diplomacy of the Undeclared War with France, 1797–1801* (New York: Scribner, 1966), 117.

5. Franciso de Miranda to Alexander Hamilton, February 7, 1798, Timothy Pickering to John Adams, August 21, 1798, *Adams Works*, 8:583–87; Alexander Hamilton to Rufus King, August 22, 1798, *Hamilton Works*, 8:505–6; Grenville to Liston, June 8, 1798, *British Instructions*, 155–60; Liston to Grenville, August 31, 1798, nos. 21 and 52, PRO FO 5; William S. Robertson, *The Life of Miranda* (Chapel Hill: University of North Carolina Press, 1929), 1:168.

6. Francisco de Miranda to John Adams, March 24, August 17, 1798, John Adams to Timothy Pickering, October 3, 1798, *Adams Works*, 8:569–72, 581–82, 600; Robert Liston to Grenville, September 27, 1798, no. 55, PRO FO 5.

7. John Adams to Timothy Pickering, October 3, 1798, *Adams Works*, 8:600.

8. Timothy Pickering to Rufus King, April 2, 1798, Arthur B. Darling, *Our Rising Empire, 1763–1803* (New Haven, CT: Yale University Press, 1940), 310.

Chapter 23: The Fate of Saint-Domingue

1. Alexander DeConde, *The Quasi-War: The Politics and Diplomacy of the Undeclared War with France, 1797–1801* (New York: Scribner, 1966), 133.

2. Alexander Hamilton to Timothy Pickering, February 21, 1799, *Hamilton Works*, 8:528–29.

3. DeConde, *Quasi-War*, 138.

4. Dudley W. Knox, ed., *Naval Documents Related to the Quasi-War with France* (Washington, DC: Government Printing Office, 1935–38), 5:318.

5. *ASPCN*, 1:384, 417, 431.

Chapter 24: Back Channels

1. Peter P. Hill, *William Vans Murray: Federalist Diplomat, the Shaping of Peace with France* (Syracuse, NY: Syracuse University Press, 1971), 426–27.

2. Dupont to Talleyrand, July 7, 1798, AAE CP EU, 50: 8–9; Pierre Jolly, *Du Pont de Nemours, Soldat de la Liberté* (Paris: Presses Universitaires de France, 1956), 189–94; Samuel E. Morrison, "Dupont, Talleyrand, and the French Spoilations," *Massachusetts Society Proceedings* 49 (1915–16), 268–73.

3. The quote appears in the margin of Rufus King to Alexander Hamilton, September 23, 1798, *Hamilton Works*, 6:359–60. The comments themselves appear in Joseph Charles, *Origins of the American Party System: Three Essays* (New York: Harper & Row, 1956).

4. Talleyrand to Pichon, August 28, 1798, *ASPFR*, 2:241–42.

5. Talleyrand to Pichon, September 28, 1798, *ASPFR*, 2:239–40; Alexander DeConde, *The Quasi-War: The Politics and Diplomacy of the Undeclared War with France, 1797–1801* (New York: Scribner, 1966), 158–60.

6. Murray to Timothy Pickering, October 5, 1798, Diplomatic Dispatches, The Netherlands, vol. 4, no. 61, State Department, National Archives.

7. DeConde, *Quasi-War*, 160.

8. Quoted in ibid., 161.

9. Ibid., 165.

10. George Washington to Reverend Blackwell, November 3, 1798, *Washington Writings*, 37:18–20.

11. DeConde, *Quasi-War*, 165–68; Manning J. Dauer, *The Adams Federalists* (Baltimore: Johns Hopkins University Press, 1952), 225.

12. *Presidential Messages*, 1:261–65.

13. Hamilton to Otis Grey, December 27, 1798, January 26, 1799, *Hamilton Works*, 6:379–80, 390–92.

14. John Adams to Abigail Adams, January 1, 1799, quoted in DeConde, *Quasi-War*, 171.

15. Joel Barlow to George Washington, October 2, 1798, *Washington Writings*, 19:560–63.

Chapter 25: The Quasi-War

1. Alexander DeConde, *The Quasi-War: The Politics and Diplomacy of the Undeclared Naval War with France, 1797–1801* (New York: Scribner, 1966); Michael Palmer, *Stoddert's War: Naval Operations during the Quasi-War with France, 1798–1801* (Columbia: University of South Carolina Press, 1987).

2. Dudley W. Knox, ed., *Naval Documents Related to the Quasi-War with France* (Washington, DC: Government Printing Office, 1935–38), 2:326–27, 356–58.

3. Palmer, *Stoddert's War*, 55, 87, 130, 131, 235, 236.

4. Report of the Secretary of State, January 18, 1799, ASPFR, 2:232.

5. Knox, *Quasi-War*, 4:313–14.

Chapter 26: British Depredations and American Honor

1. Michael Palmer, *Stoddert's War: Naval Operations during the Quasi-War with France, 1798–1801* (Columbia: University of South Carolina Press, 1987), 64.

2. Palmer, *Stoddert's War*, 63–64.

3. Alexander DeConde, *The Quasi-War: The Politics and Diplomacy of the Undeclared War with France, 1797–1801* (New York: Scribner, 1966), 203.

4. Bradford Perkins, *The First Rapprochement: England and the United States, 1795–1805* (Berkeley: University of California Press, 1967), 124–25; DeConde, *Quasi-War*, 204–6.

Chapter 27: Settling Scores with France

1. William G. Brown, *The Life of Oliver Ellsworth* (New York: Da Capo Press, 1970).

2. Blackwell P. Robinson, *William R. Davie* (Chapel Hill: University of North Carolina, 1957).

3. Alexander DeConde, "The Role of William Vans Murray in the Peace Negotiations Between France and the United States, 1800," *Huntington Library Quarterly* 15 (February 1952): 185–94; Alexander DeConde, "William Vans Murray and the Diplomacy of Peace, 1797–1800," *Maryland Historical Quarterly* 48 (March 1953): 1–26.

4. Talleyrand, Report to the Consuls of the Republic, Stanley Elkins and Eric McKitrick, *The Age of Federalism: The Early American Republic, 1788–1800* (New York: Oxford University Press, 1993), 681.

5. Brown, *Ellsworth*, 284; George H. Hoar, ed., "A Famous Fete," *Proceedings of the American Antiquarian Society* 12 (April 1898): 240–59.

6. Alexander DeConde, *The Quasi-War: The Politics and Diplomacy of the Undeclared War with France, 1797–1801* (New York: Scribner, 1966), 265–66.

Chapter 28: The 1800 Election

1. McHenry to John McHenry Jr., May 20, 1800, May 31, 1800, *Hamilton Papers*, 24:507–12.

2. Alexander Hamilton to John Adams, August 1, October 1, 1800, "A Letter from Alexander Hamilton Concerning the Public Conduct and Character of John Adams, Esq., President of the United States," *Hamilton Papers*, 25:51, 125–26, 186–234.

3. Herbert S. Parmet and Marie B. Hecht, *Aaron Burr: Portrait of an Ambitious Man* (New York: Macmillan, 1967); Nancy Isenberg, *Fallen Founder: The Life of Aaron Burr* (New York: Viking, 2007).

4. Hamilton to Bayard, January 16, 1801, *Hamilton Papers*, 25:319–20.

5. Dumas Malone, *Jefferson the President, First Term, 1801–1805* (Boston: Little, Brown, 1970), 12.

6. Kenneth C. Martis, *The Historical Atlas of Political Parties in the United States* (New York: Macmillan, 1989).

7. Manning J. Duer, *The Adams Federalists* (Baltimore: Johns Hopkins University Press, 1953); Clinton Rossiter, "The Legacy of John Adams," *Yale Review* 45 (Summer 1957): 528–50; Stephen G. Kurtz, *The Presidency of John Adams: The Collapse of Federalism, 1795–1800* (Philadelphia: University of Pennsylvania Press, 1957); John M. Allison, *Adams and Jefferson: The Story of a Friendship* (Norman: University of Oklahoma Press, 1966); Lisle A. Rose, *Prologue to Democracy: The Federalists in the South, 1789–1800* (Lexington: University of Kentucky Press, 1968); Ralph Adams Brown, *The Presidency of John Adams* (Lawrence: University of Kansas Press, 1975).

Consequences

1. Report on the Public Credit, January 9, 1790, *Hamilton Papers*, 6:106.

2. George Washington to Earl of Buchan, April 22, 1793, *Washington Writings*, 12:282–84; Alexander Hamilton analysis of the Nootka Sound Crisis, September 15, 1790, *Hamilton Works*, 4:20–49.

3. John Adams to Thomas Jefferson, September 4, 1785, Lester J. Cappon, ed., *The Adams-Jefferson Letters: The Complete Correspondence between Thomas Jefferson and Abigail and John Adams*, (Chapel Hill: University of North Carolina Press, 1959), 1:61.

4. John Jay to John Adams, September 6, 1785, *Jay Correspondence*, 3:164–65.

5. Benjamin Wright, ed., *The Federalist Papers: The Famous Papers on the Principles of American Government* (New York: Barnes and Noble, 1961), 11:137.

6. *Annals*, 1st Cong., 1st sess., 1:214, 256; Thomas Jefferson to John Langdon, September 11, 1785, *Jefferson Papers*, 8:512–13.

Index

About the Author

Dr. William Nester is a professor in the Department of Government and Politics at St. John's University in New York. He is the author of thirty previous books on different aspects of international relations.